W9-BYG-764

FRUITVILLE PUBLIC LIBRARY

100 COBURN ROAD
SARASOTA, FL 34240

LEADING WOMEN

Model and
First Lady

Melania Trump

BETHANY BRYAN

Cavendish
Square
New York

Published in 2018 by Cavendish Square Publishing, LLC
243 5th Avenue, Suite 136, New York, NY 10016

Library of Congress Cataloging-in-Publication Data

Names: Bryan, Bethany, author.
Title: Melania Trump : model and first lady / Bethany Bryan.
Description: New York : Cavendish Square Publishing, 2018. | Series: Leading women | Includes bibliographical references and index.
Identifiers: LCCN 2017013876 (print) | LCCN 2017016002 (ebook) | ISBN 9781502631800 (library bound)| ISBN 9781502634122 (pbk.) | ISBN 9781502631817 (E-book)
Subjects: LCSH: Trump, Melania--Juvenile literature. | Presidents' spouses--United States--Biography--Juvenile literature.
Classification: LCC E914.T77 (ebook) | LCC E914.T77 B79 2018 (print) | DDC 973.933092 [B] --dc23
LC record available at https://lccn.loc.gov/2017013876

Editorial Director: David McNamara
Editor: Jodyanne Benson
Associate Art Director: Amy Greenan
Designer: Renni Johnson
Production Coordinator: Karol Szymczuk
Photo Research: J8 Media

The photographs in this book are used by permission and through the courtesy of: cover MediaPunch Inc/Alamy Stock Photo; p. 1, 29 The White House via Getty Images; p. 4 Neilson Barnard/ WireImage/Getty Images; p. 8 STR/AFP/Getty Images; p. 13 MANDEL NGAN/AFP/Getty Images; p. 15 Jacques Langevin/Sygma/Sygma via Getty Images; p. 18 Dimitrios Kambouris/ WireImage/Getty Images; p. 26, 33, 39 Ron Galella/WireImage/Getty Images; p. 30 Bachrach/Getty Images; p. 36 Wojtek Laski/Getty Images; p. 42 John Roca/NY Daily News Archive via Getty Images; p. 46 Bennett Raglin/Getty Images; p. 48 Christopher Gregory/Getty Images; p. 51 Anadolu Agency/ Getty Images; p. 53 Scott Olson/Getty Images; p. 64 Chip Somodevilla/Getty Images; p. 67 Drew Angerer/Getty Images; p. 71 Spencer Platt/Getty Images; p. 75 Samuel Corum/Anadolu Agency/ Getty Images; p. 76 Pete Marovich - Pool/Getty Images; p. 78 dpa picture alliance/Alamy Stock Photo; p. 81 Leonard McCombe/The LIFE Picture Collection/Getty Images; p. 86 huseyin ozdemir1/ Shutterstock.com.

Printed in the United States of America

CONTENTS

CHAPTER ONE

Big Dreams

It was the evening of November 8, 2016, and although the event was technically a party, the mood at the event was mixed. For weeks, most news sources had been calling the presidential election in favor of former secretary of state Hillary Clinton over her rival, businessman and former reality television star Donald Trump. But as the election results rolled in, the mood at the Hilton Hotel in New York City slowly improved. At 10:53 p.m. EST, Trump took the key **battleground state** of Florida and its twenty-nine electoral votes, and as midnight approached, more and more states went in favor of the unlikely, widely criticized Republican nominee. What seemed like an impossibility just days before was suddenly looking probable. By around 2:30 a.m. on November 9, the electoral votes from Wisconsin were

Election night 2016 was a happy one for Melania Trump, who saw her husband win the presidential race.

officially counted, and Donald Trump was officially declared the president-elect of the United States.

This win did more than skyrocket a businessman to the role of world leader. It would make Melania Trump, a former model and Donald Trump's third wife, the first foreign-born First Lady since Louisa Adams, wife of John Quincy Adams, the sixth president. The media set to work, discussing her qualifications for the job and analyzing her election night outfit, a Ralph Lauren jumpsuit costing $4,000 that either intentionally or unintentionally mirrored a white pantsuit worn recently by Clinton during the third and final presidential debate. (The press could only speculate on the wardrobe choice.) Melania, who had stayed mostly out of the limelight, giving interviews on occasion and only weighing in on her husband's campaign via **Twitter** when she felt he was being unfairly criticized, was suddenly the focus of a lot more attention than ever before. Who was Melania Trump? Was she ready to be First Lady of the United States (or FLOTUS), following in the footsteps of the departing FLOTUS, Michelle Obama—a lawyer and Harvard graduate? Was it a role Melania Trump even wanted? Whether she was ready or not, Melania Trump had a brand-new job—and a new life—headed her way.

Life in Sevnica

Melanija Knavs was born on April 26, 1970, in Novo Mesto, Slovenia (which, at the time, was still part of the **communist** nation of Yugoslavia). She grew up in Sevnica, an industrial community on the bank of the Sava River. Many residents of Sevnica, including both of Melanija's parents, were employed by a state-run textile factory. Melanija's mother, Amalija, worked as a pattern maker, and Viktor, Melanija's father, worked as a driver for one of the factory's directors. (He later went on to sell cars and motorcycles.) Working at the factory was considered a good job. The family wasn't wealthy, but they weren't poor. They lived in a modest apartment building right next to the primary school Melanija and her sister, Ines, attended.

Viktor was a member of the Communist Party, putting him in the minority among Slovenians at the time—only 5 percent considered themselves communists. Aligning with the Communist Party was beneficial to the Knavs family. During shortages, when specific goods were being rationed, Viktor was able to get items that other people couldn't, like car parts and fuel.

Slovenia Today

Slovenia is a small country, only about 7,827 square miles (20,271 square kilometers), making it slightly smaller than the state of New Jersey. It has a population of almost two million people. Slovenia shares a border with Austria, Hungary, Croatia, and Italy. The port cities of Izola, Koper, and Piran on the Adriatic Sea open

Melanija Knavs (*second from right*) began modeling in fashion shows staged by the factory where her mother worked.

Slovenia up for trade with neighboring Italy and other European nations.

Despite having been part of the Austro-Hungarian Empire for several centuries and then part of Yugoslavia for a good portion of the century that followed the empire's dissolution, Slovenia has maintained a unique culture and language. In Slovenia, the primary language is Slovene. Family is important in Slovenia, and there is a strong importance placed on maintaining one's home and surroundings. It's because of this that parks and streets are well maintained, allowing tourism to thrive. Travelers to Slovenia are often entranced by the peaks of the Julian Alps and green forest regions, which cover over 50 percent of Slovenia. Architecture and design are an important part of Slovenian culture. Castles dating back centuries are important destinations for many visitors.

Manufacturing is a large part of the Slovenian economy. There's a large automotive industry, along with production of wood and metal products, chemicals, textiles, paper, and electronics. Farmers primarily grow wheat, corn, sugar beets, barley, apples, and pears. Slovenian cuisine is heavily influenced by German, Austrian, Hungarian, and Italian cooking. Meats and sausages, seafood, pasta, potatoes, and fresh fruits and vegetables are often used in Slovenian cooking.

Art and Big Dreams

Melanija was a good student. She was frequently busy reading when friends wanted her to come out and play. She was good at art and loved to make things with her hands. In a 2016 interview with the Associated Press (AP), childhood friend Mirjana Jelancic said Melanija was "an excellent student, very organized, disciplined, with very decent manners ... We would never hear her swear or say anything bad to anyone."[1] Melanija, a diplomat at heart, was always the one who worked out disputes between friends on the playground, according to Jelancic.

From an early age, Melanija was very interested in fashion and beauty. She frequently knitted and made her own clothes. Melanija, her older sister, Ines, and other friends—also children of factory employees—would take

Life Under Communist Rule

In the United States, where capitalism is the basis for the economic and political system, people work in order to buy things and support themselves. Businesses compete to sell the most products at the best price, keeping manufacturing costs low and turning the best possible profit. Some businesses fail, and some succeed. Under capitalism, people are free to make their own decisions about spending. Their spending supports businesses.

In a political system ruled by communism, people work in order to support the good of the nation. They are assigned specific tasks—farming, manufacturing goods, maintaining public places, teaching, etc. Then goods and food products are distributed among the people fairly, at least in theory.

But the reality of living in a communist regime is different. In order to keep its citizens compliant, communist governments often resort to **indoctrination** tactics. According to a May 2016 article from the *Independent* on life in communist-ruled North Korea, the most important classroom

part in fashion shows organized by the factory. These events would be attended by government officials, with one such fashion show taking place at one of the most luxurious hotels in Belgrade (the capital of Yugoslavia) at the time, the Hotel Jugoslavija. Melanija, Ines, and their friends loved the attention. But it was Melanija lesson that students learn is the life of the ruling family and current leader Kim Jong Un. Citizens are cut off from Western television, newspapers, or anything representative of culture outside of North Korea. This also occurred under Stalin's rule in the Union of Soviet Socialist Republics (USSR) in the twentieth century.

Of course, this type of rule is an extreme example of communism, a mixture of communism and a dictatorship. Stalin's successor, Nikita Khrushchev, allowed, even promoted, consumerism. This was all under firm control, of course, with the best products only made available to government officials. Quality of life in communist nations varies under different leadership and economic conditions, and according to trade restrictions with other nations. The 1970s Slovenia of Melanija Knav's childhood was only loosely under communist control, as Yugoslavia at that time allowed each nation in its union the ability to rule itself independently.

who decided she wanted to become a model. She loved to draw designs for clothing and tried to pick up new fashion ideas from trade show magazines her mother had. She wanted to always look her best. Melanija was naturally ambitious, and she had big dreams that would take her out of Sevnica, she hoped, for good.

The Evolution of Yugoslavia

World War I officially ended in 1918, and although the fighting was over, Europe was still deeply entrenched in chaos. The Austro-Hungarian Empire was dissolved, leaving the nations of Serbia, Croatia, and Slovenia divided internally and open to invasion by Italy. The three nations, along with Montenegro, Macedonia, Bosnia and Herzegovina, and some territory formerly held by Austria and Hungary, formed a union called the Kingdom of the Serbs, Croats, and Slovenes. In 1929, this became the nation of Yugoslavia, ruled by royal dictator King Alexander I. But many people were unhappy with this arrangement. They felt that ruling power had simply moved from Vienna to Belgrade, but they still didn't have any say. Parts of the nation were thriving, and others were suffering. The union of these independent states was meant to give them strength, but the continued chaos over the years only weakened the country.

In 1941, amid World War II, Yugoslavia fell quickly to an attack by Nazi Germany and its fascist ally, Italy. Thousands of civilians were killed in the invasion. Yugoslavia was now under Axis control, divided up among Germany, Hungary, and Italy.

At the end of World War II, when the Axis powers lay in defeat, the Yugoslav Union was as divided as it ever had been before. Josip Broz Tito, who had helped liberate Yugoslavia from German rule, established a new government. Yugoslavia was now a communist nation and would remain one until it was officially dissolved in 2003.

Viktor and Amalija Knavs, Melania Trump's parents—seen here in 2017—worked hard to give their two daughters a good education.

Pursuit of a Dream

Viktor and Amalija Knavs wanted their girls to succeed. They saved up a little money and rented out an apartment in Ljubljana, Slovenia's capital, when Melanija was about fifteen. Even though primary schooling in Slovenia ended for the girls when they were in their mid-teens, the move would allow them to continue their education through a technical high school. It was at this school that Melanija studied industrial design. Her hard work eventually paid off, and she was accepted at the University of Ljubljana, in the architecture program. However, Melanija still had her heart set on modeling.

In 1987, at the age of seventeen, Melanija met a famous Slovenian fashion photographer named Stane

Jerko. Jerko offered to take some pictures of Melanija to help get her modeling career off the ground. These photos helped her to get a few small modeling gigs and work acting in television commercials. Her first modeling job was for Vezenine Bled, a prominent Yugoslavian textile factory that was later destroyed as war raged in that part of Europe.

At some point over those few years of early success, Melanija changed her name to the more Germanized Melania Knauss. The name would help her to leave her Slovenian roots behind and have broader professional appeal in other European countries.

In 1992, Melania took part in a modeling contest for the Slovenian women's magazine *Jana*. The goal of the magazine's Look of the Year contest was to give Slovenian girls and women the opportunity to launch modeling careers, a goal that had always seemed out of reach in the past to women who lived under communist rule. The models who took the top three spots in the contest would be given modeling contracts in Paris, Milan, and Vienna—a ticket out of Slovenia. The contest was extremely competitive. "Melania was one of the girls who participated at the event," said *Jana* editor Bernarda Jeklin in an interview with the Associated Press in 2016. "I wouldn't say that Melania was outstanding. She was quiet, introverted. But what I remember were her dangerous, tiger-like green eyes."[2]

These Slovenian soldiers stand atop a captured Yugoslavian tank.

Melania came in second place in the contest, and although she was devastated at not having won first place, she had gained something valuable: Melania had a modeling contract in Milan. She dropped out of the university architecture program and packed her bags.

Unrest in Slovenia

Around the time that Melania Knauss decided to pursue her modeling career outside of Slovenia, the country and some of the other nations surrounding it were in a state of unrest. Josip Broz Tito had ruled the nation of Yugoslavia from the end of World War II until his death in 1980, and after his death, the six republics that made up Yugoslavia had all slowly become more independent. Slovenia, particularly, was a thriving nation where communism maintained only a loose hold over its citizens and economy; the nation had been gradually becoming more democratic. When Slobodan Milošević, the president of Serbia, announced that he planned to once again centralize the Yugoslavian government, this didn't sit well with the countries that had been functioning as independent states. Slovenia held its first multiparty elections in 1990 and formed the Slovenian Assembly, which would act as the country's parliament. In response, Milošević took control of the Yugoslav army, ordered troops to march on the Slovenian borders, and launched a propaganda campaign that he hoped would embolden Serbians living in Slovenia to rise up against the Slovenian forces. His plan was not successful, however, because, in 1991, Slovenia and Croatia officially declared their independence from Yugoslavia. Macedonia would follow soon after, declaring its independence in September that year.

In late June of 1991, the Independence War (also known as the Ten-Day War) broke out, as the Yugoslav army attempted to invade Slovenia. The goal was to reach the larger cities and get them back under Yugoslavian control, but the Slovenian people had been preparing for this invasion. They had been stockpiling arms and building barricades at border crossings. Slovenian militia used simple defense tactics and **guerrilla warfare**, never attacking the Yugoslav forces head on. They employed antitank weapons, and as a result, the tank-heavy Yugoslav army was halted in their tracks. By July 4, all border crossings were under Slovenian control, and Yugoslav forces were in retreat. Slovenia was officially an independent state.

Although Slovenia escaped with minimal casualties, it's important to remember that other countries engaged in war against Yugoslav forces were not so lucky. Thousands were killed in Croatia after the nation declared independence from Yugoslavia. The state of Bosnia was made up of a larger variety of people with a wider range of beliefs than in Slovenia. Bosnian Serbs were resistant to the independence movement, while Bosnian Muslims and Croats supported it. Soon a civil war broke out in Bosnia. Bosnian Muslims and Croats were driven from their homes by the Bosnian Serb Army and slaughtered through a campaign of ethnic cleansing. Around one hundred thousand people were killed in this act of genocide that took place between 1992 and 1995. In 2006, the last states of the former Yugoslavia, Serbia and Montenegro, became independent nations.

CHAPTER TWO

Life of a Model

In a speech during a campaign stop in Pennsylvania in 2016, Melania Trump said, "As a young **entrepreneur**, I wanted to follow my dream to a place where freedom and opportunity were in abundance. So of course, I came here [to America]." She added, "Living and working in America was a true blessing, but I wanted something more. I wanted to be an American."[1]

Starting Out

Building a career as a model can be a difficult task for even the most physically attractive and dedicated of women. It's extremely competitive. You have to work

Melania Knauss struggled in her early modeling career, but she finally found her foothold after moving to New York.

hard and stay fit, and sometimes, even if you have the looks and the ambition, you still might be rejected by the top agencies.

Much of Melania's modeling career during the 1990s has been lost to time, to protect either her privacy or the business exploits of the man who would eventually become her husband. However, the 2016 book *Melania Trump: The Inside Story; The Potential First Lady*—written by two Slovenian journalists, Bojan Požar and Igor Omerza—tried to shed some light on Melania's years as a model, despite being rejected upon its release as "lies" by the Trump organization.

According to the book, with the *Jana* modeling contract in her pocket, Melania left Slovenia and moved to Milan, where her career got off to a difficult start. Once in the historic Italian city—home of designers Dolce & Gabbana, Prada, and Armani, among others— she was signed by the Riccardo Gay modeling agency. Gay was a well-known fashion scout in Milan with connections to several successful Italian businessmen and politicians. These famous friends would throw parties, and Gay would send some of his agency's models over to attend the parties and act as "arm candy" for the wealthy male guests. According to an anonymous source who worked for the Riccardo Gay agency at the time, models could choose not to attend, but the ones who did received more modeling gigs. Many argue that this practice of hiring out models as party guests takes away a model's body autonomy and ability to manage her own career and self-interests. Melania soon left the agency in search of one that better suited her needs.

She finally traveled to Vienna in 1993 to meet Wolfgang Schwarz, founder of Look Models International. Melania was determined to be one of the models Schwarz represented, so she walked up to his offices and knocked on the door—a bold move for a virtual unknown in the world of fashion.

Schwarz had once been a model himself. He knew the business inside and out. (He is often credited with jumpstarting the careers of **supermodels** Naomi Campbell and Linda Evangelista.) Schwarz believed that the most important attributes of a model were a strong personality and an excellent work ethic. Being beautiful was just the icing on the cake to Schwarz. He didn't believe that one could teach the attributes of being a good model; it was something you either had or you didn't. He also believed that a good model should already be fluent in some of the languages she would be expected to speak overseas. Schwarz also carried a bias against models from Eastern Europe, writing them off as more interested in maintaining a party lifestyle than putting in the hard work required in order to become a model. Being from Slovenia, Melania fell into that category and had to work harder to prove herself to Schwarz. Although Schwarz got Melania some gigs, he thought she was lacking that extra "something special." He thought she was cold and lacked energy in her work.

But Melania was determined to make it. Later in 1993, her luck changed, and she landed a gig back in Milan with famed designers Gucci and Valentino. This was followed by a fashion show for Pino Lancetti, an Italian designer known for his designs based around famous works of art. In 1996, Melania appeared on the cover of the Spanish edition of *Harper's Bazaar*. Things were looking up. Melania started getting gigs through the Metropolitan agency run by Paolo Zampolli, a modeling agent based in New York, the fashion capital of the United States. Zampolli urged Melania to relocate to New York. He even helped to arrange her paperwork to do so—an issue that would come up again years later. Melania was ready to leave her European roots and make the move to America.

The Rise of the Supermodels

Making it as a model in the United States in the 1990s was no easy task. The field was competitive, with more beautiful women arriving in New York every day, all trying to get a foot in the door of the fashion industry. Designers' needs were constantly changing, and so were their standards. A model who found more than enough work one month might find herself jobless the next because of a slight weight gain or a perceived bad

The Challenges of Modeling

Modeling is all about having the "ideal body." The "Gibson girl" of the early 1900s had a small waist and hourglass curves. By the 1960s, models like Twiggy and Jean Shrimpton had the "ideal body," with their slender figures and doll-like facial features. During the 1990s, models were expected to be small and thin, like supermodel Kate Moss.

Many models of the 1990s struggled to maintain the necessary weight. This led to cases of anorexia and bulimia in the fashion industry. Some models resorted to using drugs to help control their weight. These issues continue to exist in the modeling industry today.

Models also struggle to find quality representation. A model cannot go out and find gigs on her own. She has to work with an agency, and some agencies take a large cut, whether or not the model is finding regular work. In an article on the Model Alliance website, one model says, "The day I signed with a modeling agency in New York, a manager sat me down to explain the terms of our working relationship. I was excited to be there, even a bit giddy to be signing a modeling contract, but not so much as to miss the crucial terms: in exchange for exclusive representation and a standard 20 percent commission from my earnings, the agency would promote and manage my modeling career."[2] A model's earnings can fluctuate a great deal from one month to the next, and they are often not provided with health insurance coverage or any kind of retirement plan.

attitude. The level at which you could consider yourself a successful model was also rising.

In January of 1990, a photographer named Peter Lindbergh shot a cover for British *Vogue* that would launch models Naomi Campbell, Cindy Crawford, Christy Turlington, Linda Evangelista, and Tatjana Patitz into stardom. These five women are considered the original "supermodels." Rather than simply being faces on the cover of *Vogue* and *Glamour*, supermodels were celebrities in their own right. Singer George Michael booked the models for the video for his song "Freedom." They became the faces of Armani, Versace, and Calvin Klein. They acted in movies and on television. Supermodels dated rock stars and actors and showed up on the pages of celebrity gossip magazines for their "diva-like behavior" and extravagant lifestyles. Models were also commanding more money for their work. They were more in control of what jobs they accepted and what was expected of them. Before "brand-building" was a buzzword, supermodels like Kate Moss, Elle Macpherson, and Kathy Ireland were building their brand.

In the mid-1990s, Kate Moss arrived on the scene as the new face of Calvin Klein. Throughout the 1980s and early 1990s, the tall, buxom "glamazon" model had been the ideal. But Moss was small and very thin. She had crooked teeth. Many in the fashion industry liked that her looks were so unique. Moss's ads for Calvin Klein were provocative. Sometimes she appeared topless or even nude in the ads. "Modeling" had become less about the clothes and more about the woman selling them, to a point where customers didn't even need to see the clothes to buy the brand.

Few models during the 1990s succeeded on the level of those who could call themselves supermodels. This was a brand-new level of fame, and a lot of women and girls from all over the world wanted in.

A New Life in New York

Melania Knauss officially moved to New York in 1996 (1995, according to *Melania Trump: The Inside Story*). She signed a lease on her first New York apartment, just off of Union Square in Manhattan. By the time she moved to New York, Melania was getting gigs through both Metropolitan and Elite Model Management. It was through Paolo Zampolli that she met fellow model Edit Molnar, who was originally from Hungary and, like Melania, was trying to get her career started in New York. Edit and Melania became friends, despite the difference in their personalities. Melania was extremely disciplined, while her friend loved to go out and party. Melania was more soft-spoken and reserved, while Edit was outgoing.

According to Molnar, who shared her memories in *Melania Trump: The Inside Story*, Melania worked hard at every modeling gig she got. She stayed away from

Melania Knauss at the 2000 VH1 Vogue Fashion Awards

drugs and alcohol and worked hard to maintain her body. She was undemanding and completely professional. Designers liked working with her. But most of the work that Melania did was for ads and for catalogs. No one knew the names of catalog models. Melania wasn't a supermodel. She made plenty of money, but she wasn't a name or a brand. This bothered Melania. She didn't just want people looking at her photographs. She wanted them to know her name. She was missing out on the fame part of being a successful model.

A Chance Meeting

In 1998, Melania Knauss attended a party at the Kit Kat Club in New York. She was twenty-eight at the time. The party was hosted by Melania's friend and sometimes-manager Paolo Zampolli. Zampolli was known for his lavish parties, which often featured wild animals like alligators and tiger cubs. His parties were always attended by lots of beautiful models, according to a 2016 *New York Times* article. Zampolli knew businessman Donald Trump through their shared enjoyment of the New York nightclub scene and some business interaction, so naturally Trump would be in attendance. It was at this party that Melania Knauss met Donald Trump for the first time.

Donald Trump was a New York icon, a businessman who had achieved a level of fame in the 1980s and early 1990s for his brash, ego-laden interviews with the press, his bestselling book *The Art of the Deal*, and later, his widely publicized divorce from his first wife, Ivana. Trump had invested in real estate in New York City during the 1970s when the economy was suffering, financed through a loan given to him by his father, and when the economy improved during the

1980s, his fortune grew. Trump used this fortune to invest in casinos in Atlantic City, airlines, hotels, and other properties, applying the "Trump" name to each of them—a name that, he believed, carried an air of success and wealth. During the 1990s, a recession hit, making it difficult for Trump to stay ahead of the debts accrued by so many investments, and several of his holdings were forced to declare bankruptcy. At one point, he owed over $110 million to creditors—some sources put this number at almost $1 billion. But by 1995, he had bounced back, through a number of loans from investors who trusted the Trump brand. He celebrated his recovered success with another book, *The Art of the Comeback*, in 1997.

In 1998, Trump was fifty-two years old, had just separated from his second wife, Marla Maples, and was actually on a date with another woman when he attended Paolo Zampolli's Kit Kat Club soiree. The woman on Trump's arm for the party was Celina Midelfart, a Norwegian heiress. Said Trump in an interview about their first meeting, "I saw Melania and I said, 'Who is that?' … She was a very successful model. She was terrific. I tried to get her number, and she wouldn't give it to me." In the same interview, Melania said, "I had heard he was a ladies' man, and so I said, 'I'm not one of the ladies.'"[3]

Instead, Melania insisted on getting his number, and Trump gave her all of the phone numbers he had. After she returned from a modeling job in the Caribbean, she called him.

From the Magazine Covers to the Official Portrait

A First Lady typically has an official portrait, and these portraits can generate some controversy. For instance, Michelle Obama's first official portrait led to some controversy over her sleeveless dress. Some people found it to be too casual and off-season. It is no surprise, however, that First Lady Melania Trump's first official portrait was a bit more glamorous.

Melania's picture was taken in the West Sitting Hall of the White House. Regine Mahaux, the photographer, is well known for her portraits of celebrities. She has also taken many pictures of Melania, including high-glamour photographs. Melania Trump chose a black tuxedo-style jacket with a sequined neckerchief. The portrait also features Melania in soft focus with her large engagement ring displayed on her ring finger. While some people expressed how beautiful Melania looked in the portrait, others felt the portrait looked too airbrushed.

The White House Historical Association features a slideshow of official First Lady portraits. Both Edith Roosevelt and Helen Taft were shown in a more glamorous style, making Melania Trump's portrait not the first glamour shot.

Early in April 2017, Melania Trump released her official portrait as First Lady, shown here

CHAPTER THREE

Finding Fame, Success, and Happiness

onald Trump was born on June 14, 1946, the fourth of the five children of Frederick and Mary Trump. Trump's father was a real estate developer who had made his fortune building and operating apartments for middle-income residents across Brooklyn, Queens, and Staten Island in New York City. But to understand the life and career of Donald Trump, we must look back at where his fortune originated.

Donald Trump rose to fame in the 1980s as a successful real estate tycoon.

The Trump Organization

Donald Trump's grandfather, Friedrich, had immigrated to the United States from Germany in the late 1800s to avoid being drafted by the German army. He moved to Seattle, Washington, where he opened a restaurant and hotel. In 1892, he became a United States citizen and eventually changed his name to the more Americanized "Frederick." The newly named Frederick Trump moved to Yukon Territory to take advantage of the gold rush there, building a restaurant and hotel to accommodate the miners. These prospects made the elder Trump incredibly wealthy by early twentieth-century standards. On a visit to Germany, he met and married Elizabeth Christ. The younger Frederick Trump, Donald's father, was born in 1905.

The younger Frederick Trump (often known simply as Fred) had a head for business from an early age. He hadn't even turned twenty-one yet when he and his mother, Elizabeth, founded the E. Trump and Sons construction company. Throngs of immigrants were moving to New York during the early twentieth century. War veterans were returning to America to find that they couldn't afford to own a home. In 1934, President Franklin Roosevelt created the Federal Housing Administration to help fix the housing industry, putting construction workers back to work and helping low-income individuals and families to own their own homes.

Fred and Mary Trump at the Police League Awards Dinner in 1999

Fred Trump saw the potential in this and took advantage of the program's loan **subsidies** to build housing. In the mid-1930s, Fred Trump met Mary MacLeod, a Scottish immigrant. The couple married and settled in Jamaica, Queens, where Donald Trump's older siblings, Maryanne, Freddy, and Elizabeth, were born.

When World War II broke out, the family moved to Virginia, where Fred would build apartments for the US Navy. Fred Trump knew a business opportunity when he saw one. After the war, the family moved back to New York, where Donald was born in 1946, followed by the youngest sibling, Robert. Fred Trump felt that it was important to get his family involved in his business as soon as they were old enough. The eldest son, Freddy, was meant to be the heir of his father's business and fortune, but Freddy struggled with meeting his father's expectations and soon fell victim to alcohol abuse. Eventually, Freddy left real estate and became a pilot for Trans World Airlines, a job he loved. After Donald Trump graduated from college and began to rise in the Trump Organization, it became apparent that he was better suited to work in his father's real estate business than his older brother had been. By 1971, Donald was placed in charge of the company.

Freddy Trump passed away in 1981 at the age of forty-three, a victim of long-term alcoholism. Freddy's death and struggle with alcohol are the reasons Donald Trump cites for never consuming alcohol himself.

Despite the outward success of the business, the Trumps' business practices were often called into question. The Trump Organization boasted that it built quality homes at a good price, but rumors began to circulate as early as the 1950s that Trump's apartment homes did not accommodate African American tenants. According to a June 2016 article on the *Gothamist*, folk singer Woody Guthrie was once a tenant in one of the Trump buildings, and he even wrote a song about the alleged racism. According to the same article, supers and rental agents would tell black potential tenants that an apartment had already been rented or raise the rate to an unaffordable level. In the early 1970s, the United States government sued the Trumps for these unfair practices. At the time, the younger Trump said, "They are absolutely ridiculous. We never have discriminated, and we never would. There have been a number of local actions against us, and we've won them all. We were charged with discrimination, and we proved in court that we did not discriminate."[1] The Trumps contested the suit, but they later agreed to change how they rented to potential tenants.

Donald Trump's Rise to Fame

Before Donald Trump took the reins of the family business, the Trumps had primarily invested in real estate outside of Manhattan. Manhattan real estate was more expensive, making it more of a gamble to find success there. Luckily, the poor economy of the 1970s, followed by economic growth of the 1980s, took land prices up drastically, making anyone who owned land in Manhattan significantly richer. Donald Trump invested at the right time, and it was this decision that took the Trump Organization from moderate success to a vast fortune.

In 1980, Donald Trump became a celebrity in his own right when he was interviewed by journalist Tom Brokaw. Trump was thirty-three years old at the time and beginning to become a successful developer in his own right. More interviews followed, and throughout the 1980s, the world saw Donald Trump go from a

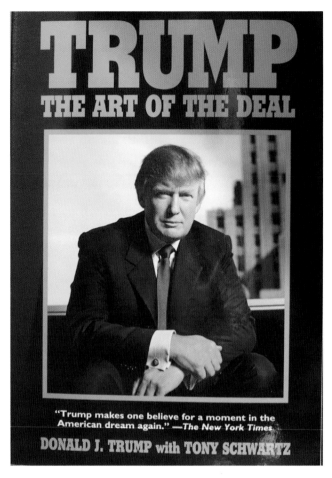

Donald Trump's *The Art of the Deal* became a best seller in the 1980s and rose again in popularity during Trump's presidential run.

simple businessman to a celebrity. He became celebrity gossip fodder in the early 1990s for his highly publicized divorce from his first wife, Ivana. News agencies and gossip magazines followed Donald Trump through career highs and lows. But Trump's success in the 1980s was unfortunately starting to slip.

Daily Life in Trump Tower

Before Donald Trump moved to the White House, his home and his business office were located at 725 Fifth Avenue in Manhattan, better known as Trump Tower. He lived there with his wife, Melania, and their son, Barron. The decoration of the three-story penthouse that occupies the top three floors of the building was inspired by the Palace of Versailles, the French royal palace. The apartment is decorated with 24-karat gold and marble. The ceilings are covered with murals and chandeliers. Trump had resided there since the building was completed in 1983. Before his run for the presidency, he ran his business from his office on the twenty-sixth floor of the building, waking up around 5:00 a.m. and arriving in his office around 8:00 a.m. Trump only sleeps about four hours per night, even after assuming the presidency.

The Trump Tower website boasts that the building is sixty-eight stories tall, but in reality, it's only fifty-eight floors. Trump estimates the floor count in order to exaggerate the height of the tower. For instance, he estimated that the first real floor was the thirtieth floor based on average ceiling heights, but that estimate is ten floors higher than what it should have been labeled. Trump Tower residents pay into the millions of dollars to buy homes in the building.

In 2017, on the eve of Trump's inauguration, New Yorkers gathered at Trump Tower to protest, making life difficult for the building's residents and those running businesses in the building.

Trump Trouble

In 1987, Donald Trump took control of the Taj Mahal casino in Atlantic City. The project had sat unfinished for a while after the death of the company's owner, and Trump felt that he was just the businessman to finish the job. He just needed to raise enough money to finish the $1 billion project, and in order to do that, he needed to convince some banks to loan him the money at a reasonable interest rate.

At last, Trump was approved for the loans, but at a high interest rate: 14 percent. The casino was finally completed, and the Taj Mahal, the world's largest hotel-casino at the time, opened in 1990. But the casino's earnings were not enough to keep up with the high interest payments. In order to keep the business afloat, Donald Trump had to make arrangements with several of his lenders. He gave up 50 percent of his ownership share in the hotel, sold his airline and a 220-foot (67 m) yacht, and agreed to limits on his personal spending.

In 1992, Trump's other two Atlantic City casinos, Trump's Castle and Trump Plaza, were forced into bankruptcy. Later that year, the Trump Plaza Hotel in New York also declared bankruptcy. During his long career, Trump has also seen the failure of Trump Steaks, Trump Vodka, Tour de Trump (a bicycle race), and other ventures.

Donald Trump and Melania Knauss pose together at New York's Radio
City Music Hall in 1999, early in their relationship.

Melania in the Limelight

When Melania Knauss met and dated Donald Trump, Trump's business dealings were looking up, but he was separated but not yet divorced from his second wife, Marla Maples. Suddenly, Melania was in the limelight for the first time, the girlfriend of a wealthy New York celebrity. The public had witnessed two very public separations from Trump, so anyone he dated was destined to be the target of a lot of speculation and gossip.

One of the first rumors, of course, was that the twenty-eight-year-old was only after Donald Trump for his fortune. Said Melania in an interview in response to those early claims, "I think you can't be with the person if it's not love, if they don't satisfy you. You can't hug a beautiful apartment. You can't hug an airplane. You can't talk to them."[2]

A Big Cover Shoot

With her face in the press, Melania was finding success and fame she had never experienced before. Suddenly, everyone wanted to take her picture. In January 2000, Melania got an offer to pose for the cover and an article in British *GQ*. "We were bombarded by requests to shoot Melania," said *GQ* editor Dylan Jones in an interview with the *Hollywood Reporter* in 2016 when asked about the experience.[3]

The photos were taken around and aboard Trump's own private jet and featured Melania in a campy "Bond girl" storyline. The resulting photos were considered racy by some standards. In one, Melania appeared nude, lying on a fur rug. In another, she was mostly topless, with an open, jewel-filled briefcase.

Of course, appearing nude or partially nude is quite common among the modeling community and can even be empowering for the models, if they are made to feel comfortable and the work is done in a respectful and **consensual** manner. Models Rosie Huntington-Whiteley, Bella Hadid, Chrissy Teigen, and others posed nude for a *W* magazine shoot in 2015. Alessandra Ambrosio appeared in the nude in a 2016 issue of *GQ Brasil*. According to a 2016 British *GQ* article about the shoot that Melania did, she is quite proud of her work.

An Extravagant Affair

Melania's relationship with Donald Trump was tumultuous in the beginning. The couple broke up a few times, though they always got back together soon after. Finally, in 2001, Melania moved to Trump Tower. In 2004, Trump proposed to Melania during the Costume Institute Gala. The ring was a $1.5 million diamond ring. Of their engagement, Trump said at the time, "She's shown she can be the woman behind me. We're together five years, and these five years for whatever reasons have been my most successful. I have to imagine she had something to do with that."[4]

Donald Trump and Melania Knauss married in 2005 at a lavish ceremony at Mar-a-Lago, Trump's Florida resort.

Donald Trump is no stranger to extravagance, and his wedding to Melania Knauss was no exception. The wedding took place at Mar-a-Lago, Trump's Palm Beach estate and resort club.

Melania's dress was a Dior-designed, hand-beaded gown made of almost 100 yards (91 m) of white satin. A 13-foot (4 m) train followed Melania down the aisle on her big day. The dress cost over $100,000. Her sister, Ines, acted as her maid of honor, and Trump's sons, Donald Jr. and Eric, acted as his best men.

Celebrities in attendance included Bill and Hillary Clinton, Heidi Klum, Barbara Walters, Katie Couric, Billy Joel, Arnold Schwarzenegger, P. Diddy, Anna Wintour, Derek Jeter, Shaquille O'Neal, and countless others.

The seven-tier cake weighed in at over 200 pounds (90 kilograms), stood 5 feet (1.5 m) tall, and was covered with over two thousand handmade sugar flowers. An elaborate system of wires and platforms had to be constructed to hold the cake upright, and because of the wires, guests were unable to eat any of the cake. Luckily, smaller, more edible chocolate truffle cakes were served as well. The main cake was the most expensive wedding cake in history at the time, according to a 2016 article on Brides.com. (Today, the "most expensive wedding cake" honor is held by the eight-tier cake created for the wedding of Prince William and Kate Middleton.)

The Apprentice

The same year that Donald Trump proposed to Melania Knauss (2004), his star was on the rise again, this time as the host of *The Apprentice*. The show was created by Mark Burnett, who had risen to success on the back of his hit reality series *Survivor*. Competitors would engage in challenges that they hoped showed them to be business savvy, and at the end of each episode, one competitor who had not performed well would be dismissed by Donald Trump himself. The final contestant would earn a job within the Trump Organization.

At the time that Burnett came to Trump with his idea for the show, Trump was not a fan of reality television. But he agreed once Burnett assured him that it wouldn't take up much of the businessman's time, and the show could be filmed inside Trump Tower. "My jet's going to be in every episode," he said, according to a *Fortune* article. "The Taj is going to be featured. Even if it doesn't get ratings, it's still going to be great for my brand."[5]

Twenty million viewers tuned in for the first episode of the show. By the end of the first season, that number would be twenty-seven million. Season 1 winner Bill Rancic was hired by Trump to oversee the construction of Trump Tower Chicago. Rancic later went on to star in reality television programs of his own: *We Mean Business*, *Kitchen Casino*, and others. Rancic said of Trump in an interview with CNBC in 2016, "He was incredible to me and changed my life. I give him a lot of the credit. If it wasn't for him, I wouldn't have met my wife and things would have been different for me. He gave me the opportunity of a lifetime. I got to watch him from the inside and I was able to see how he works and how he does deals and how he was able to negotiate in difficult times."[6]

Barron Trump

Barron Trump was born in 2006. Seeing the resemblance early on, Melania took to calling him "Little Donald." Even as a baby, Barron occupied an entire floor in his parents' famous apartment, complete with its own living room, kitchen, and nanny's quarters. He played with his own cars and helicopters (toys, of course). He was even, on occasion, caught drawing on walls in the Trumps' penthouse apartment, but Melania laughed it off since it was his own floor.

In an interview with *Parenting* when Barron was six, Melania described her life as a parent:

I am a full-time mom; that is my first job. The most important job ever. I started my business when he started school. When he is in school I do my meetings, my sketches, and everything else. I cook him breakfast. Bring him to school. Pick him up. Prepare his lunch. I spend the afternoon with him. Sometimes I have obligations, but I also think children need to see a parent do what her passion is. It is a good example for a child. So the child can find passion as well and follow that passion in the future.[7]

Melania Trump: Businesswoman

A lot of things had changed since a little girl named Melanija got excited about modeling the latest fashions back in Slovenia in the 1970s. Melania Trump had found that success she had longed for back then. She was now a wife and a mother. She lived in a penthouse apartment overlooking Fifth Avenue. But, despite all that success, the ambition had never gone away. Now, it seemed that the business world was calling Melania's name.

In 2010, Melania announced that she would begin selling her own line of jewelry—Melania Timepieces & Jewelry—on QVC. The jewelry, designed by Melania herself, was also priced for the average customer, with the most expensive piece selling at about $200. The collection

Melania Trump wears a watch and ring from her own collection.

sold out in forty-five minutes, according to a 2015 article on the *Daily Beast*.

In a 2012 appearance on QVC, Melania said of her jewelry line, "It's my passion for beauty and fashion to design something for women across the country that they could have fun with—something that they could afford that you could easily buy on QVC—and really special pieces that you could wear from morning until night."[8]

In 2012, Melania launched her own line of beauty products. The anti-aging creams were infused with caviar and were sold at high-end department stores like Lord & Taylor. According to a 2016 article on Racked.com, Melania had been working for years to get the idea off the ground, hiring a chemist and a skin expert to help put together the formula. But ultimately the skin care line launch did not go as well as the jewelry sales did.

Melania had signed a manufacturing deal with a company called New Sunshine LLC. The company also manufactured Kardashian Glow for the reality television clan, so the company seemed to be reputable. But shortly after the contract was signed, New Sunshine was in financial trouble. The company's two main investors, John Menard and Steve Hilbert, had lost money on some other investments and had resorted to lawsuits and countersuits in order to reclaim some of their lost money. Eventually the pair sued Melania in order to try to break her contract. The skin care line was shut down before it had even gotten off the ground.

CHAPTER FOUR

A Run at the Presidency

I n 1988, Donald Trump appeared on *The Oprah Winfrey Show* to talk about his first book, *The Art of the Deal.* He also shared some of his ideas on United States foreign policy. It was during that interview that Trump first publicly weighed the possibility of running for president. His response to Winfrey's question about the possibility was, "Probably not. But I do get tired of seeing the country get ripped off."[1]

Donald and Melania Trump are shown here at Trump Tower on the day Trump announced his presidential run.

Announcement at Trump Tower

On June 16, 2015, a group of supporters gathered at Trump Tower for a big announcement from Trump himself. He was officially running for president, and he was doing so on the Republican ticket. As he rode down the golden escalator of Trump Tower on his way to addressing his supporters, he waved and gave thumbs up to the eager crowd. Melania was at his side for the event.

"Our country is in serious trouble," Trump said in his speech. "When was the last time anybody saw us beating, let's say, China in a trade deal? They kill us. I beat China all the time. All the time." Trump was unhappy with what he saw as poor leadership on the part of then the current United States president, Barack Obama. He spoke out against the Affordable Care Act, calling it a "disaster." He spoke out against the dangers of Islamic terrorism and how the country needed to wipe out ISIS as soon as possible. "I am officially running ... for president of the United States," Trump went on to say, "and we are going to make our country great again."[2]

This wasn't Trump's first run at the presidency. In 2000, he ran for the nomination on the Reform Party ticket, receiving more than fifteen thousand votes in the California primary. In 2012, Trump mulled another run, but ultimately he threw his support behind Republican nominee Mitt Romney.

Unfortunately for the Trump campaign, Trump's announcement speech was met with controversy that

After Donald Trump called for banning Muslim immigrants from entry into the United States, several protests broke out across the country.

spread quickly across social media. In the speech, Trump had made comments about the people of Mexico that many considered to be racist. He also went on to say that in order to prevent Mexican people from entering the country illegally, he would authorize the building of a wall, and he would find a way to make the country of Mexico pay for it. He didn't offer any insight as to how the wall would be built, but this proposal drew a strong response from anti-immigration far-right supporters.

Latinos living in the United States were quick to react. Lisa Navarrete of the National Council of La Raza (a civil rights organization for Hispanic people) said in an interview with the *Guardian*, "This is a man who has a pathological need for attention."[3] She went on to call Trump's referral to Mexican people as "rapists" offensive.

The comments had further consequences. Univision, an American Spanish-language network, announced it would not be airing the Miss USA Pageant, an organization that Trump owned at the time. This was followed shortly by an even larger blow. It seemed that NBC would be cutting ties with Trump as well. After fourteen seasons of *The Apprentice*, Trump would not be returning as host. Initial reports said that Trump was fired for the comments, but he disputed that later, saying that he had "fired himself" because the network didn't want him to run for president.

Despite her show of outward support, Melania wasn't so sure about her husband's presidential bid, according to a 2016 article in the *Washington Post*. According to Trump, when he approached Melania with the idea of him running for president, she said, "We have such a great life. Why do you want to do this?"[4] In 2000, during Trump's earlier bid at the presidency, the couple broke up briefly, and some believe that it was because Trump was too focused on his campaign. She clarified her opinion, however, in a 2015 interview on *20/20*, saying, "I encouraged him because I know what he will do and what he can do for America. He loves the American people and he wants to help them."[5]

A Bumpy Campaign Trail

Before Donald Trump could officially run for the office of the presidency against the Democratic nominee, he

The first Republican debate for the 2016 election took place on August 6, 2015, in Cleveland, Ohio.

would first have to win the Republican nomination, and there were many high-profile Republican candidates standing between him and his goal. The first Republican debate took place on August 6, 2015. In the debate, Trump faced former Florida governor Jeb Bush, Wisconsin governor Scott Walker, former Arkansas governor Mike Huckabee, former neurosurgeon Ben Carson, Texas senator Ted Cruz, Florida senator Marco Rubio, Kentucky senator Rand Paul, New Jersey governor Chris Christie, and Ohio governor John Kasich. Trump and Carson were the only candidates without significant experience as a politician.

Debates give voters a chance to find out where their candidates stand on particular issues, so it's important to stay focused on the topics. To do this, moderators keep track of time limits and steer candidates back to the topic. One of the moderators of the first debate was Megyn Kelly, then a correspondent for Fox News. During the debate, Kelly said to Trump, "You've called

Celebrities Who Have Run for Office

Donald Trump is not the first celebrity to run for political office. Historically, celebrities might run for office for the publicity or because they are actually interested in getting into politics. Let's look at some of the most famous examples.

Clay Aiken: This singer and *American Idol* runner-up ran for Congress in 2014 in his home state of North Carolina. Aiken lost his bid for the seat to Representative Renee Ellmers.

Sonny Bono: Singer and half of the famed duo Sonny and Cher, Sonny Bono ran for mayor of Palm Springs, California, during the 1980s and won. In 1994, he ran for Congress and was elected. Tragically, his political career was cut short by a fatal skiing accident. Bono's wife, Mary, ran for the vacated seat and served until 2013.

Clint Eastwood: In 1986, actor and director Clint Eastwood ran for mayor of Carmel, California, and won. During his two-year term, Eastwood approved an application for an ice cream parlor, thereby fulfilling one of his campaign promises.

Al Franken: *Saturday Night Live* alum and comedian Al Franken ran for a Minnesota Senate seat in 2008 and won. Franken graduated in 1973 from Harvard with a degree in political science.

Ronald Reagan: Probably the most famous example of a celebrity who made a successful transition to politics is former actor and two-term president Ronald Reagan. Previously he had served two terms as governor of California from 1967 to 1975.

Arnold Schwarzenegger: Facing a tough financial situation in California at the time, action star Arnold Schwarzenegger ran for governor of the state in 2003. He served two terms, after which time he went back to acting. He appeared in *The Expendables* and its sequels and later went on to briefly take over hosting *The Apprentice*.

women you don't like 'fat pigs,' 'dogs,' 'slobs,' and 'disgusting animals.' ... Does that sound to you like the temperament of a man we should elect as president, and how will you answer the charge from Hillary Clinton, who [is] likely to be the Democratic nominee, that you are part of the war on women?"[6]

This question irritated Trump, and he reacted later in an interview with CNN by saying, "She gets out and she starts asking me all sorts of ridiculous questions. You could see there was blood coming out of her eyes, blood coming out of her wherever. In my opinion, she was off base."[7] Women across the country were unsettled by Trump's remarks, and questions about the businessman's treatment of women began to come to the surface. Since women represent 50 percent of the American voting public, Trump would need to work hard to make sure he appealed favorably to that base. Of the criticism, he said to CBS's *State of the Union* in 2015, "I cherish women. I want to help women. I'm going to do things for women that no other candidate will be able to do."[8] Many people looked to Melania Trump to weigh in, as a woman and the wife of the candidate. She had stayed mostly out of the limelight during the early part of the campaign, but that was about to change.

Melania Faces Public Scrutiny

Throughout Trump's campaign, Melania stayed out of the limelight. But her explanation for her absence was simple: she needed to be a good mom to her son. During an interview with Barbara Walters on *20/20*, Melania said, "I support my husband 100 percent, but … we have a nine-year-old son together, Barron, and I'm raising him."[9]

But questions often arise about a candidate's spouse, and sometimes it's impossible to keep to yourself and maintain a private life. If the other side can find out some information they can use to damage an opponent's reputation, things that family members have left in the past might start coming to the surface.

During his campaign, Trump made it clear that he did not support illegal immigration, no matter the reason. Melania was an immigrant herself, having left Europe for America in 1996. In order to live and find work in the United States, an individual must apply for a **work visa**. Melania arrived in August of 1996 with a tourist visa, and she didn't receive her work visa until October of that year. Therefore, any work she was paid for during those few months—around $20,000, according to the Associated Press—violated United States immigration law. Michael J. Wilkes, an attorney who represented the Trump Organization, released a letter in 2016 denying that Mrs. Trump was ever in the nation illegally. But many were still skeptical since Melania Trump didn't release her immigration files to the public. In the midst of this controversy, it was also revealed by the *New York Post* that Melania Trump had been photographed in the nude for the magazine *Max* in 1996. (Some early reports said the photo shoot had taken place in 1995, apparently further proof that she was in the country illegally as early as 1995, but an article from *Politico* revealed that the magazine that featured the photographs was the February 1997 issue.) As mentioned previously, a nude photo shoot is nothing new for a professional model, but for the wife of a politician running on the conservative ticket, this was a bombshell. Said Donald Trump in response to the outrage, "Melania was one of the most successful models, and she did many photo shoots, including for covers and major magazines. This was a picture taken for a European magazine prior to my knowing Melania. In Europe, pictures like this are very fashionable and common."[10]

Welcome to the RNC

During an election year, both the Republican and Democratic parties hold official conventions at which they formally announce their presidential candidate. The 2016 **Republican National Convention (RNC)** was held in Cleveland in late July.

Despite generally staying out of the limelight, Melania Trump was scheduled to speak on the first night of the convention. It's a long-standing tradition for the potential First Lady to speak in front of the convention, a tradition that began with Eleanor Roosevelt in 1940. Roosevelt's speech, which called for unity in the Democratic Party, helped Franklin Delano Roosevelt, or FDR, win the election that would usher in his third term in office. Only a few potential First Ladies haven't taken this opportunity to endorse their husbands—or wife, in Bill Clinton's case during the Democratic National Convention in 2016.

With her speech, Melania sought to convey her own story, that of an immigrant who moved to America in order to succeed, and what she learned on that journey. The speech was met with applause during the convention. Unfortunately, others who were watching noticed something else.

"OMG. Melania. That was literally a whole line from Michelle Obama 2012," tweeted freelance journalist Jarrett Hill (@JarrettHill) as he watched the speech unfold.[11]

Over the next hour, Hill's followers spread the word. It appeared that Melania Trump had **plagiarized** a few paragraphs of Michelle Obama's DNC speech from 2008. (Hill initially misidentified which of Michelle Obama's convention speeches had been plagiarized.)

Here is an excerpt from Melania's speech:

From a young age, my parents impressed on me the values that you work hard for what you want in life, that your word is your bond and you do what you say and keep your promise, that you treat people with respect. They taught and showed me values and morals in their daily lives. That is a lesson that I continue to pass along to our son.[12]

Here is an excerpt from Michelle Obama's speech:

> *And Barack and I were raised with so many of the same values: that you work hard for what you want in life; that your word is your bond and you do what you say you're going to do; that you treat people with dignity and respect, even if you don't know them, and even if you don't agree with them.*[13]

In response to the claims, the Trump campaign issued a statement. Trump speech writer Meredith McIver took the blame for the mistake, alleging that she had helped Melania Trump write the speech, using Obama's speech for inspiration, and that some of the original words had made their way into the final product. McIver submitted her resignation, but Donald Trump rejected it, calling the issue a simple mistake.

The public was not as forgiving. The facetious #FamousMelaniaTrumpQuotes hashtag, popularized by actor Jesse Williams, popped up almost immediately, with the public attributing popular quotes to Melania Trump. For instance, one Twitter user called @brownsugar7878 tweeted, "I have a dream, that one day, my four little children will need ot [sic] be judged by the color of their skin," referencing the immortal words of Martin Luther King Jr.'s "I Have a Dream" speech.[14]

Whether or not the plagiarism was intentional, when the Republican National Convention was over, the candidate from the Republican Party had been announced, and it was Donald Trump.

The Trump Children

Donald Trump likes to get his children involved in his business as soon as they are old enough. As he campaigned for the presidency, his children were at his side. Let's take a look at some of their contributions to the Trump campaign and presidency.

Donald Trump, Jr. is the oldest of Trump's children. Donald Jr. remained a close adviser to his father throughout the campaign. Along with his brother Eric, Donald Jr. took over the bulk of the day-to-day handling of his father's business.

Ivanka Trump is the second child of Donald and Ivana Trump. At the RNC, she introduced her father with a speech that sought to humanize him as a father and a businessman. After the election, Ivanka took an unpaid role working in the White House as a close adviser to the president.

Eric Trump works alongside his brother Donald Jr. running the Trump Organization in their father's absence.

Tiffany Trump is the only child of Donald Trump and Marla Maples. Out of the spotlight for a number of years after her parents' divorce, Tiffany made an appearance at the RNC to provide support to her father. After college, she pursued law school.

Accusations of Sexism and Sexual Assault

In early October 2016, word of a video recording was making the rounds across the media. In it, Donald Trump was recorded, with a hot microphone on the *Access*

Hollywood bus, speaking with show host Billy Bush about kissing and groping women against their will. "When you're a star, they let you do it," he said. Upon noticing *Days of Our Lives* actress Arianne Zucker standing nearby, Trump said, "I better use some Tic Tacs, just in case I start kissing her. You know I'm automatically attracted to beautiful—I just start kissing them. It's like a magnet. Just kiss. I don't even wait."[15] In the same audio recording, Trump talks about a failed attempt to seduce an unnamed married woman. The recording was made in 2005, just months after his marriage to Melania. But this wasn't the first time Donald Trump had said or done hurtful, offensive, or **misogynistic** things to women. During a 2015 court appearance for a Florida real estate lawsuit, a female attorney requested a recess so she could go pump breast milk for her three-month-old baby. "You're disgusting," Trump remarked.[16]

Melania Trump often responds to the media in a calm way that suggests her disappointment in what her husband says, but at the same time she also conveys her affirmation of his assertiveness and boldness. She responded to the recording from *Access Hollywood*, stating, "The words my husband used are unacceptable and offensive to me. This does not represent the man that I know. He has the heart and mind of a leader. I hope people will accept his apology, as I have, and focus on the important issues facing our nation in the world."[17] Donald Trump responded by saying, "I never said I'm a perfect person, nor pretended to be someone that I'm not. I've said and done things I regret, and the words released today on this more than a decade-old video are one of them. Anyone who knows me knows these words don't reflect who I am."[18]

But the accusations soon began to move past words. Soon after the tape was released by the media, a woman named Jessica Leeds stepped forward, in an article in the *New York Times*, to claim that Trump had once tried to grope her breasts and put a hand up her skirt while the two sat side by side on a flight to New York in the early 1980s.

In the same article, Rachel Crooks, who had once worked as a receptionist for a business in Trump Tower, alleged that Trump had kissed her on the mouth when she tried to introduce herself in 2005. Several more women came forward with similar accusations over the next few weeks. But Melania Trump refused to find truth in any of the claims. She even insisted that the women were the ones at fault. "I see many, many women coming to him and giving phone numbers and, you know, want to work for him," Melania said in an interview with Anderson Cooper in October 2016. "And they know he's married … [They do it] in front of me." Later in the interview she said, "My husband is kind, and he's a gentleman, and he would never do that … Everything was organized and put together to hurt him, to hurt his candidacy."[19]

CHAPTER FIVE

The Votes Are In

Election Day 2016 was a tense one, but it was not without its light-hearted moments. That morning, Donald and Melania Trump headed to the polls, like the rest of the country, to cast their votes. The cameras caught Donald Trump peering over the divide to, many guessed, make sure that his wife was voting for him and not his opponent. The photo went viral. But Trump had nothing to worry about. Within the next twenty-four hours, he would be declared the president-elect of the United States.

Across the nation, Trump supporters celebrated. Many people who had felt forgotten during the previous eight years under a Democratic presidency felt like they were finally going to have their say. Happy voters wore their

Donald Trump celebrates his defeat of Democratic candidate Hillary Clinton to become the forty-fifth president of the United States.

red "Make America Great Again" hats to celebratory rallies and waved signs. But not everyone was happy with the outcome of the 2016 election. Opponents pointed to Trump's previous comments and treatment of women. Others were concerned that his comments about undocumented immigrants were going to embolden American nationalists, leading to an uptick in hate crimes.

Inauguration Day

Donald Trump's inauguration took place on January 20, 2017, with thousands of people in attendance. Melania held the Bible as her husband took the oath of office. Once, during the inauguration, Donald Trump turned to speak to his wife, and when he turned away, it appeared that her smile dropped into a frown, prompting many to question whether or not Melania Trump was truly happy in her new position. A #SaveMelania hashtag soon popped up on Twitter. But neither the new First Lady nor the president weighed in with any explanation of the somber mood of the occasion.

The day following the inauguration was also a busy one in Washington, DC, as almost 500,000 women (and men) showed up in the nation's capital to protest. According to a *New York Times* article, three times as many people showed up to protest than showed up for the inauguration itself. This directly opposed the new president's own claims that 1.5 million people had attended his inauguration. Faced with the numbers,

Melania and son Barron are shown as Donald Trump is inaugurated.

President Trump lashed out against the news media, saying that journalists are "among the most dishonest human beings on earth."[1] Sean Spicer, the White House press secretary, followed up on the president's claims, saying that news organizations "had deliberately misstated the size of the crowd at Mr. Trump's inauguration on Friday in an attempt to sow divisions at a time when Mr. Trump was trying to unify the country," according to the *New York Times*.[2]

In the president's hometown of New York, tens of thousands of self-proclaimed "Nasty Women"—a reference to a comment that Donald Trump had made about Hillary Clinton during the final presidential debate—and men supportive of the cause gathered around Trump Tower to protest. Even a small village in **Nova Scotia** got in on the action, arranging a women's protest of its own—twelve women, two men, and a toddler were in attendance. President Trump spoke out against the protests, saying via Twitter, "Watched protests yesterday but was under the impression that we just had an election! Why didn't these people vote? Celebs hurt cause badly."[3]

The Code of Ethics

When a new president—or any elected official, for that matter—is sworn into office, he or she must adapt to the code of ethics of an elected official. As government employees, elected officials must avoid certain financial conflicts of interest and gifts or payments for their work that might be perceived as bribes. They must also avoid exploiting their position or resources to influence others.

This code of ethics also applies to the First Lady. On January 21, 2017, as the president and First Lady were settling into their respective roles, the White House website was updated to provide links to some of the latest policies, cabinet appointments, and biographies for the new administration. Under Melania Trump's biography, her modeling work was listed, along with information about her jewelry line at QVC. This was a violation of the code of ethics because a First Lady cannot use her position to turn a profit or promote her personal brand. Almost immediately, the information was taken down.

This code of ethics is handled by the US Office of Government Ethics. It's this group's job to make sure that the president operates within his power restraints. This power check is part of what keeps the three branches of government on equal footing and ensures that the president is not acting on behalf of any outside organization or business.

Before taking on the role of the presidency, the president-elect must rid himself of these conflicts of interest. To do this, most presidents have **blind trusts**, where an independent party takes over the official's investment portfolio. He or she can no longer see or engage in business practices outside of the government. (This is a practice begun by Lyndon B. Johnson in 1963.) But this is a complicated thing for Donald Trump to do because his investments are tied into his personal brand. The Trump name is what keeps his businesses operating. So rather than putting his investments in a blind trust, Donald Trump turned over control of his business empire to his two oldest sons, Donald Jr. and Eric. This isn't a foolproof plan, however, because nothing prevents the Trump sons from calling their father and discussing the day-to-day operation of the business, except a solemn promise that they won't.

The Cost of Safety

Moving into the White House is a tradition over two hundred years in the making. In many ways, it's like

The Birth and Reinvention of a Brand

Branding is, simply put, a way for businesses to create long-term relationships with customers using emotional appeal. When actor Isaiah Mustafa showed up wearing a towel in the first of several advertisements for Old Spice, this was part of a reinvention of the Old Spice brand. According to a 2010 *Adweek* article, Old Spice sales were suffering. Many people associated the brand with the past and older men. The product had been around since 1938, and customers had built an air of nostalgia around it, which doesn't help to attract new customers. Old Spice was competing with a brand that was appealing to much younger men, Axe, so it had to find a fresh, new way to sell the product. Advertising insiders called this the "swaggering" of Old Spice. The new ad spots starring Isaiah Mustafa sent Old Spice sales skyrocketing within a month.

When a company needs to get the word out there about its product, the company will rely on social media to help build the brand. Everything tweeted out by that account must be "on brand," or aligning with the values of the company, so that customers start to associate it with a good product. If a company makes socks with cats on them, the brand must be cute, like a cat, and comforting, like a sock. Therefore, that company's Twitter account might post cat memes and encourage followers to tweet about their favorite pair of socks. The Trump brand is based around the appeal of wealth and success.

After Trump's inauguration, his New York building required security.

moving to a new home for anyone, except the departing president moves out on the same day the incoming president moves in. The new First Family may choose to redecorate the residence to their tastes, picking out wallpaper or paint colors, furniture, and whatever else will make the White House feel like home. This is a task traditionally taken on by the incoming First Lady.

However, in November 2016, Donald Trump announced that Melania and their son, Barron, would not be moving to the White House after his inauguration—at least, not right away. The family wanted Barron to be able to finish out his school year in New York before making the transition to a new school. After this announcement, many parents threw their support behind

The Role of the Secret Service

When you picture the Secret Service, images of black-suited individuals running alongside a motorcade might pop into your mind, or a brave soul leaping between the president and a bullet. But the Secret Service has a long history that has traditionally involved more than just keeping the president safe.

Originally, the Secret Service was a division of the Treasury Department. Their sole mission? To help crack down on money counterfeiting, which was running rampant in the 1860s, when the Secret Service came to be. But then, in 1901, President William McKinley was assassinated–the third sitting president to die under these circumstances in thirty-six years–and at that point, the Secret Service took on the additional role of protecting the president. They also protect the rest of the First Family, the vice president and his or her family, former presidents, foreign heads of state visiting the United States, and presidential candidates.

Melania. "Good, this is what most responsible parents do with a child Barron's age," said one Twitter user, according to an article on BBC.com.[4] A *Denver Post* article even proclaimed the decision a step in the right direction for feminism. The article pointed out that "the first lady is an unpaid, unofficial government representative whose roles

The job of the Secret Service is all about prevention. Secret Service agents do meticulous research and, while on the job, watch out for threats. The Secret Service investigates these threats to determine whether or not the president's life is genuinely in danger. Additionally, the Secret Service investigates cases of identity theft, credit card fraud, and potential computer hacking issues.

Despite the danger of the job, only one Secret Service agent has ever been killed while protecting the president. In 1950, two armed Puerto Rican nationalists attempted to storm Blair House (the president's official guest house), where President Harry Truman was staying while the White House was undergoing renovations. Secret Service Officer Leslie Coffelt was shot as he attempted to block their entrance to the residence. He succumbed to his wounds that evening.

and influence are defined almost entirely in respect to her relationship with her husband."[5]

However, many critics found fault with the choice, especially when it came to the cost. Melania's choice to stay in New York would end up costing taxpayers a lot of money. The First Family requires a security detail to keep them safe. According to a *Fortune* article, security for Trump Tower, just for the time period between the election and the inauguration, cost New York City around $24 million. According to the same article, to protect just Melania and Barron Trump would cost between $127,000 and $145,000 per day. Since Trump Tower is a skyscraper and not a private residence, keeping it secure requires a more extensive form of protection and more Secret Service agents to be on duty around the clock.

In May 2017, the *New York Times* reported that Barron Trump would begin attending St. Andrew's Episcopal, a prep school in Potomac, Maryland, beginning in the fall. The announcement indicated that Melania and her son would be moving to the White House that summer, following the end of Barron's school term in New York.

Melania Trump vs. the *Daily Mail*

On August 2, 2016, the *Daily Mail*, a tabloid stationed in the United Kingdom, published an article alleging that Melania Trump once worked for an escort service. Melania wasted no time in bringing a **libel** suit against Mail Media—the company that owns the *Daily Mail*. She sought compensation of around $150 Million.

Libel is a type of defamation found in the written word, such as a blog post or news article. (If someone makes a damning statement out loud, it's called **slander**.) The person who was libeled—in this case Melania Trump—

Melania speaks at the 2017 International Women of Courage Awards.

must then prove, in court, that the statement is false and that it has caused irreparable harm. Otherwise, the author of the allegedly libelous piece of writing is protected by the First Amendment. This makes libel lawsuits, particularly for public figures, especially hard to win.

According to the *Washington Post*, the lawsuit claimed the allegations hurt her chances to establish strong business ties during her time as First Lady. Based on that language, it was interpreted that Melania had

After Donald Trump took office, he signed several executive orders, covering topics like offshore drilling, immigration, and abortion.

apparently intended to use her position to promote her brand, selling accessories, shoes, jewelry, cosmetics, and other products. But, as previously mentioned, making a profit using a political position for leverage goes against the code of ethics, so this lawsuit raised a lot of questions beyond the allegations. Richard Painter, a White House ethics counsel during the presidency of George W. Bush, said to the *Washington Post*, "There has never been a first lady of the United States who insinuated that she intended to make a lot of money because of the 'once-in-a-lifetime' opportunity of being first lady."[6]

Charles Harder, the lawyer who represented Melania Trump, released a statement that denied the allegation: "The first lady has no intention of using her position for profit and will not do so. Any statements to the contrary

are being misinterpreted."[7] Ultimately, Melania settled
the lawsuit with the *Daily Mail* in April 2017.

The President's Executive Orders

By March 6, 2017, President Trump had signed thirty-
four executive orders. An executive order is not a law, but
an "official statement from the president about how the
federal agencies he oversees are to use their resources,"
according to the *Washington Post*.[8] Historically, executive
orders have been used in many ways, both good and bad.
The Emancipation Proclamation was an executive order
in which Abraham Lincoln set a date for the release
of three million slaves. Franklin Roosevelt signed an
executive order in 1942, two weeks after the attack on
Pearl Harbor, that ordered the forced relocation of over
110,000 Japanese Americans into internment camps.

One of the more controversial of Trump's executive
orders banned people from seven majority-Muslim
countries from entering the United States for ninety
days. It was Trump's hope that this order would block
Muslim terrorists from entering the country. The ban
included many green card holders, who were in the
United States legally. Many were stopped at airports,
unable to enter the country under the new executive
order. Protests broke out across the United States. Since
Melania Trump was an immigrant herself, many looked
to the new First Lady to become their advocate in the
White House.

CHAPTER SIX

An Unfinished Legacy

Melania Trump officially became the First Lady of the United States when her husband was sworn in as the president. But what kind of First Lady will she be? Historically, First Ladies have been able to set their own course when it comes to levels of involvement, issues they want to pursue, and how they want to present themselves to the public. How will Melania measure up? What kind of **legacy** will she leave behind?

What Does a First Lady Do?

Although Martha Washington was technically the very first "First Lady," she was not known by that title during

First Lady Michelle Obama greets the new First Lady, Melania Trump, on Inauguration Day 2017.

her lifetime. (She was often called "Lady Washington.") Allegedly, President Zachary Taylor coined the term while eulogizing the late Dolley Madison during her funeral in 1849. The term did not fully take off, however, until journalist Mary C. Ames was covering the 1877 inauguration of Rutherford B. Hayes and referred to the new president's wife, Lucy, as the new "First Lady." This role is traditionally occupied by the woman who is married to the president, but that is not always the case. Harriet Lane was James Buchanan's niece and assumed the role, since the fifteenth president never married, for example, and several other presidents relied on their daughters or other female relatives to fill the role.

Over the years, the role of First Lady of the United States has come to include different tasks and different levels of involvement within a presidency. Traditionally, the First Lady is the official White House hostess and is involved with event planning. The role has changed over the years, however, mainly through the efforts of Eleanor Roosevelt. The wife of the thirty-second president expanded her role beyond domestic duties, giving press conferences, speaking out for issues that affected women and children, and working for the League of Women Voters. She even traveled overseas during World War II to speak to the troops. Since then, the First Lady tends to work for a specific cause or set of causes as part of her duties. Jackie Kennedy worked on historical preservation. Lady Bird Johnson worked for environmental issues.

Jackie Kennedy was known for having her own stylish flair.

Laura Bush spent her time on education initiatives. And Michelle Obama focused on fighting childhood obesity and promoting education for girls. As First Lady, like the First Ladies before her, Melania Trump will have the ability to pick her own cause.

An Unspoken Role

One unspoken duty that is expected of the First Lady is to maintain an air of style and glamour. Mamie Eisenhower defined the 1950s by wearing her iconic shade of pale bubblegum pink. Jackie Kennedy reinvented the fashion of the early 1960s, wearing pillbox hats, oversized sunglasses, subtle bows, and elbow-length gloves. But since the role of the First Lady is an unpaid position, her clothes are purchased out of pocket. Said former First Lady Laura Bush in her 2010 memoir, "I was amazed by the sheer number of designer clothes that I was expected to buy, like the women before me, to meet the fashion expectations for a first lady. After our first year in the White House, our accountant said to George [W. Bush], 'It costs a lot to be president,' and he was referring mainly to my clothes."[1]

Melania Trump herself has long been considered by many a fashion icon. As a former model and New York socialite, dressing impeccably has always come naturally to Melania. The pale-blue matching dress and jacket she wore to the inauguration immediately drew comparisons to one once worn by Jackie Kennedy on the day of her own husband's inauguration in 1961.

Melania Takes on Cyberbullying

In November 2016, Melania Trump announced that she would like to address cyberbullying and harassment as her main cause as First Lady. She said:

> We have to find a better way to talk to each other, to disagree with each other, to respect each other. We must find better ways to honor and support the basic goodness of our children, especially in social media. It will be one of the main focuses of my work if I'm privileged enough to become your First Lady.[2]

Many people reacted to this announcement with criticism, saying that Melania's own husband was a notorious cyberbully. In the past, Trump has tweeted what many have perceived to be inflammatory comments at many who criticize him. One of the first examples of this involved television personality Rosie O'Donnell. On December 14, 2011, Trump tweeted, "I feel sorry for Rosie's new partner in love whose parents are devastated at the thought of their daughter being with @Rosie—a true loser."[3] In 2015, his attention turned to Lauren Batchelder, a teenager who had attended a political forum in New Hampshire and said to Trump during the event, "So, maybe I'm wrong, maybe you can prove me wrong, but I don't think you're a friend to women." Erroneously believing that Batchelder was on the payroll of his Republican primary opponent Jeb Bush, Trump tweeted, "The arrogant young woman who questioned me in such a nasty fashion at No Labels yesterday was a Jeb staffer! HOW CAN HE BEAT RUSSIA & CHINA?"[4] As a result, Batchelder started receiving threats of violence from Trump supporters that continued up through Election Day 2016.

Following Melania's announcement of her anti-cyberbullying campaign, Lady Gaga (@ladygaga) tweeted in response, "to say u will stand for 'anti-bullying' is hypocrisy. Your husband is 1 of the most notorious bullies we have ever witnessed."[5] Lady Gaga, herself an anti-bullying advocate, founded the Born This Way Foundation in 2012. As of early 2017, Melania Trump had yet to pursue the cause of cyberbullying officially.

The Fight Against Cyberbullying

Since the internet has come into existence, cyberbullying has been one of the unforeseen downsides of this great achievement in global communication, particularly among children and teens. According to an article on Uknowkids.com, 43 percent of kids have been bullied online, and one out of four kids has been bullied more than once. Cyberbullying has also been blamed for several cases of teen suicide, as in the case of Megan Meier, who committed suicide in 2006 after Lori Drew, the mother of a friend of Megan's, began sending Megan abusive messages through MySpace under an assumed name.

Because cyberbullying is a fairly new concept, so are any laws that can help fight it. This makes prosecuting a cyberbullying case extremely difficult. Lori Drew was convicted of three misdemeanor counts, but she was later acquitted of the charges because she hadn't technically broken any laws.

Women's and Children's Issues

Early in 2017, Melania Trump made an appearance at Presbyterian/Weill Cornell Medical Center in New York City to read to children on National Read Across America Day. It was after this appearance that the media began to speculate that she had finally chosen a

She had only violated the MySpace terms of service, according to the court.

As of 2014, there were about twenty state laws in place to help fight cyberbullying, but if the right to free speech is protected by the First Amendment, how can a law protect the victims without violating the bully's rights? In 2013, Maryland passed the Misuse of Interactive Computer Service bill (also known as Grace's Law, after Grace McComas, a Maryland teen who committed suicide after enduring months of harassment). However, the law was seen as unconstitutional by the Maryland branch of the **American Civil Liberties Union (ACLU)**. The bill prohibits using a computer in such a way that inflicts emotional distress. The ACLU believed that this language was so broad it could result in charges against a teen making an offensive joke online, thereby violating the First Amendment. Under Grace's Law, cyberbullies could face up to a year in prison or a $500 fine.

"signature issue" to focus on during her tenure as First Lady—children's issues. According to Donald Trump, speaking at a news conference at the White House on February 16, 2017, Melania would also be focusing on women's issues. But what are the issues that women and children are facing, and how can the First Lady of the United States help? Let's take a closer look.

Syrian refugees often live in camps that don't have running water or sanitation.

What Issues Do Children Face?

Children in the United States often face poverty, abuse and mistreatment, inadequate health care, and nutrition issues, among others. Internationally, children are exploited for child labor and face the dangers of living in war-torn nations. The term "children's issues" covers a vast territory. Below are a few of the major issues facing children today, both in the United States and globally.

Child labor: Child labor laws protect most children in the United States, but in some countries, that is not the case. According to the Child Labor Coalition, in the nation of Nepal, a construction boom has led to around sixty thousand children being employed as brick makers in unregistered kilns that are not regulated by the government. Child labor is also on the rise in West Africa, where over two million children are employed by the cocoa industry. These are just small examples of some of the child labor issues that are occurring globally. Even in the United States, there remain child labor issues, despite the passage of child labor laws. According to a 2014 report from Human Rights Watch, children as young as seven may be employed by the tobacco-farming industry in the United States. This work exposes them to nicotine, pesticides, extreme heat from working outdoors, and other dangers related to farm labor.

Lack of access to clean drinking water: According to the World Water Council, 1.1 billion people worldwide do not have access to clean drinking water, and an average of 3,900 children die every day from waterborne illnesses. Water is a basic human requirement. In the United States, beginning in 2014, residents of Flint, Michigan, were left without clean drinking water because the city switched the water supply from Lake Huron to the Flint River. Studies found elevated levels of lead in the drinking water, which has led to multiple cases of lead poisoning in the children of Flint. In children, lead poisoning can lead to anemia, brain damage, and long-term developmental issues. As of early 2017, the Environmental Protection Agency continued to advise Flint residents not to drink unfiltered tap water.

Abuse, neglect, and the foster care system: In 2015, over 683,000 American children were the victims of abuse or neglect. Child protective services stepped in on 3.4 million cases of alleged abuse or neglect. On average, there are around 428,000 children in foster care in the United States, according to Childrensrights.org. Children are held in foster care for an average of two years. Many grow up and "age out" of the foster care system without ever finding a permanent home and family. In 2015, that number was over twenty thousand.

By aligning herself with organizations like the Children's Defense Fund, UNICEF, or the Trevor Project—an organization that provides support to LGBTQ teens and young adults—First Lady Melania Trump may be able to shed light on some of these issues, perhaps even leading to changes in policy.

What Are Women's Issues?

Many people in the United States believe that women have achieved equal rights. Women received the right to vote in 1920, following decades of work by the women's suffrage movement. The Equal Pay Act of 1963 was passed to help women earn the same pay as their male counterparts, at least theoretically. So what is it that women are fighting for? Lots of things! Women's rights is a vast field of issues related to education, employment, violence, and reproductive issues.

According to the ACLU, women are still making only seventy-eight cents for every dollar earned by men, and this number is worse for women of color. Black women earn only sixty-four cents, and Hispanic or Latina women earn fifty-four cents for every dollar a man earns. This is due to several loopholes in the Equal Pay Act. The wording of the law allows men to be paid more because of seniority, merit, or productivity. Therefore, a woman can make a complaint that she is being paid less because of her gender, but her employer can simply say that the male coworker is better at his job, even if that isn't necessarily true.

Additionally, women are more likely to be the victims of violent crime. One in three women will have been the victim of domestic violence within her lifetime, according to the National Coalition Against Domestic Violence. And one in five women will have been raped within her lifetime—for men, that number is one out of seventy-one. Organizations like the National Organization for Women, CARE, and RAINN are working hard to educate and advocate on behalf of women and girls.

Reproductive rights are among the most controversial of women's rights because they include access to reproductive health care, including birth control and abortion. Melania Trump has not commented publicly on her beliefs, so no one knows where she might stand on this issue. Donald Trump is publicly opposed to abortion, but that hasn't always been the case. According to a 2016 *Washington Post* article, in 1999 Donald Trump said in an NBC interview, "I'm very pro-choice. I hate the concept of abortion. I hate it. I hate everything it stands for. I cringe when I listen to people debating the subject.

The Rights of Roma Children in Slovenia

What issues are children facing in the First Lady's home country of Slovenia? Plenty, according to Humanium.org, especially when it comes to a small percentage of the Slovenian population. According to Amnesty International, there are between ten thousand and twelve thousand Roma living in the nation of Slovenia, making up about 0.5 percent of the population, but that number might be much higher. There is really no way to know because so many Slovenian Roma are considered homeless. They live in small, isolated communities. Many build homes on land they don't own and are therefore considered squatters.

The Roma descended from a group of people who immigrated to Europe from India about 1,500 years ago. Over the past several centuries, the Roma have been discriminated against, enslaved, executed, and expelled from their homes. The Roma people were one of the targets of the genocide perpetrated by Nazi Germany during World War II.

Today, in Slovenia, Roma children almost exclusively speak the Romani language—one made up of over sixty different **dialects**. In Slovenian schools, teachers do not speak their language. Therefore, many Roma children cannot get an education and continue into secondary education, which, in Slovenia, is when students train for a specific vocation. Roma people struggle to get jobs and provide for their families without an education.

But you still—I just believe in choice."[6] Melania Trump aligning herself with women's advocacy groups would help to unify women's rights between the Republican and Democratic Parties.

Her Ongoing Legacy

From a little girl in Slovenia who loved fashion and dreamed of being a model to becoming First Lady of the United States, Melania Trump has come a long way in her lifetime. Some worry that Melania doesn't speak out enough and that she is missing an opportunity to use her status to create positive change with her words and positions. But many also view Melania Trump as a feminist icon, unwilling to be ruled by the opinion of the public and strong-willed in her devotion to her son and her loyalty to her husband. Ultimately, Melania Trump is a businesswoman who has fought a great many odds to get to where she is today. She has proven that she has the ability and the reach to accomplish a great many things. Melania Trump's legacy is still to be determined. Only the future can tell us what kind of legacy the First Lady will leave behind.

Timeline

1993

Melania Knauss moves to Vienna to try her luck at landing some modeling gigs there.

1970

Melanija Knavs is born in Novo Mesto, Slovenia, to Viktor and Amalija Knavs.

1991

The Ten-Day War ends with Slovenia winning its independence from the nation of Yugoslavia.

1998

Melania Knauss meets Donald Trump at a party in New York City.

Melanija wins runner-up in the *Jana* magazine modeling competition and moves to Milan.

1992

Donald Trump makes his first run for the presidency, as part of the Reform Party. Melania Knauss poses for British *GQ* magazine.

Melanija meets famed Slovenian photographer Stane Jerko.

1987

2000

2004

Melania Knauss and Donald Trump marry at Mar-a-Lago resort in Florida. Donald Trump becomes the host of *The Apprentice*.

2017

Donald Trump is sworn in as president, and Melania Trump becomes First Lady.

2015

Donald Trump announces his intention to run for president of the United States.

Barron Trump is born.

2006

The presidential election takes place in November.

2016

The nation of Yugoslavia is officially dissolved.

2003

SOURCE NOTES

Chapter 1

1. Darko Bandic, "Melania Trump: Small-Town Slovenian Roots, Big Dreams," Associated Press, February 25, 2016, http://elections.ap.org/content/melania-trump-small-town-slovenian-roots-big-dreams.

2. Dusan Stojanovic, "Melania Trump's Slovenia Has Become a Tourist Hotspot," Associated Press, August 15, 2016, http://bigstory.ap.org/article/ec973eee0c3e40099665ff21b791539f/melania-trumps-slovenia-has-become-tourist-hotspot.

Chapter 2

1. Alicia A. Caldwell, Chad Day, and Jake Pearson, "Melania Trump Modeled in US Prior to Getting Work Visa," Associated Press, November 5, 2016, https://apnews.com/37dc7aef0ce44077930b7436be7bfd0d.

2. Ashley Mears, "Why Modeling Is, Technically Speaking, A 'Bad Job,'" Model Alliance, 2012, http://modelalliance.org/2012/1621/1621.

3. Nicola Oakley, "How Did Donald Trump Meet Wife Melania? President Was on a Date with Another Woman at the Time." *Mirror*, February 6, 2017, http://www.mirror.co.uk/3am/celebrity-news/how-donald-trump-meet-wife-9769146.

Chapter 3

1. Morris Kaplan, "Major Landlord Accused of Antiblack Bias in City," *New York Times*, October 16, 1973, http://www.

nytimes.com/1973/10/16/archives/major-landlord-accused-of-antiblack-bias-in-city-us-accuses-major.html.

2. Marissa Charles, "Melania Trump Would Be a First Lady for the Ages." *New York Post*, August 16, 2015, http://nypost.com/2015/08/16/melania-trump-would-be-a-first-lady-for-the-ages.

3. Alex Ritman, "GQ Editor Recalls Donald Trump Wife's Controversial Nude Photo Shoot," *Hollywood Reporter*, March 25, 2016, http://www.hollywoodreporter.com/news/gq-editor-recalls-donald-trump-878336.

4. Helin Jung, "A Definitive Timeline of Donald and Melania Trump's Relationship," *Cosmopolitan*, January 27, 2017, http://www.cosmopolitan.com/politics/a8646265/donald-trump-melania-trump-relationship-timeline.

5. Marc Fisher and Michael Kranish, "The Inside Story of How 'The Apprentice' Rescued Donald Trump," *Fortune*, September 8, 2016, http://fortune.com/2016/09/08/donald-trump-the-apprentice-burnett.

6. Andrea Park, "Bill and Giuliana Rancic Open Up on Trump, Kids, Cancer," CBS News, January 6, 2016, http://www.cbsnews.com/news/bill-and-giuliana-rancic-open-up-on-trump-kids-cancer.

7. Sabrina James, "Melania Trump Juggles Motherhood, Marriage, and a Career Just Like Us," *Parenting*, 2011, http://www.parenting.com/blogs/hip-mama/melania-trump-shares-her-1-parenting-tip-and-secrets-lasting-marriage.

8. David Ferguson, "Redesigned White House Website Plugs Melania Trump's QVC Jewelry Line," *Raw Story*, January 20, 2017, http://www.rawstory.com/2017/01/redesigned-white-house-website-plugs-melania-trumps-qvc-jewelry-line.

Chapter 4

1. "Oprah Winfrey Interviews Donald Trump in 1988," YouTube video posted by Andrew Philbrick, July 30, 2015, https://www.youtube.com/watch?v=GZpMJeynBeg.

2. "Here's Donald Trump's Presidential Announcement Speech," *Time*, June 16, 2015, http://time.com/3923128/donald-trump-announcement-speech.

3. Adam Gabbatt, "Donald Trump's Tirade on Mexico's 'Drugs and Rapists' Outrages US Latinos," *Guardian*, June 16, 2015, https://www.theguardian.com/us-news/2015/jun/16/donald-trump-mexico-presidential-speech-latino-hispanic.

4. Bob Woodward and Robert Costa, "In a Revealing Interview, Trump Predicts a 'Massive Recession' but Intends to Eliminate the National Debt in 8 Years," *Washington Post*, April 2, 2016, https://www.washingtonpost.com/politics/in-turmoil-or-triumph-donald-trump-stands-alone/2016/04/02/8c0619b6-f8d6-11e5-a3ce-f06b5ba21f33_story.html?postshare=6561459637742585&tid=ss_tw&utm_term=.8bdd9417d831.

5. "Donald Trump's Wife Melania on Their Marriage, His Campaign: Part 2," YouTube video posted by ABC News, November 21, 2015, https://www.youtube.com/watch?v=lgYTCHrWkxI.

6. Aaron Blake, "Here Are the Megyn Kelly Questions That Donald Trump Is Still Sore About," *Washington Post*, January 26, 2016, https://www.washingtonpost.com/news/the-fix/wp/2016/01/26/here-are-the-megyn-kelly-questions-that-donald-trump-is-still-sore-about/?utm_term=.eec312b6bedc.

7. Philip Rucker, "Trump Says Fox's Megyn Kelly Had 'Blood Coming Out of Her Wherever,'" *Washington Post*, August 8, 2015, https://www.washingtonpost.com/news/post-politics/wp/2015/08/07/trump-says-foxs-megyn-kelly-had-blood-coming-out-of-her-wherever/?utm_term=.884fa6a547e3.

8. Gregory Krieg, "12 Times Donald Trump Declared His 'Respect' For Women," CNN, October 7, 2016, http://www.cnn.com/2016/10/07/politics/donald-trump-respect-women.

9. "Donald Trump's Wife Melania on Their Marriage, His Campaign: Part 2."

10. "Donald Trump Responds to Melania's Newly-Surfaced Racy Photo Shoot." Fox News, August 1, 2016, http://www.foxnews.com/entertainment/2016/08/01/donald-trump-responds-to-melanias-newly-surfaced-racy-photo-shoot.html.

11. Elisha Brown, "How a Freelance Journalist Broke the Melania Trump Plagiarism Story in 3 Tweets," *Vox*, July 21, 2016, http://www.vox.com/2016/7/21/12247504/jarrett-hill-melania-trump-plagiarism.

12. Hillary E. Crawford, "Transcript of Melania Trump's RNC Speech Shows a Side of Her America Has Yet to See," *Bustle*, July 18, 2016, https://www.bustle.com/articles/173441-transcript-of-melania-trumps-rnc-speech-shows-a-side-of-her-america-has-yet-to-see.

13. Josh Lowe, "Michelle Obama and Melania Trump: Compare the Speeches," *Newsweek*, July 19, 2016, http://www.newsweek.com/melania-trump-michelle-obama-plagarism-compare-speeches-full-text-481779.

14. Josh Elliott, "'Famous Melania Trump Quotes': Twitter Skewers 'Plagiarized' Speech," CTV News, July 19, 2016, http://www.ctvnews.ca/world/famous-melania-trump-quotes-twitter-skewers-plagiarized-speech-1.2992610.

15. "Transcript: Donald Trump's Taped Comments About Women," *New York Times*, October 8, 2016, https://www.nytimes.com/2016/10/08/us/donald-trump-tape-transcript.html.

16. Jeremy Diamond, "Lawyer: Donald Trump Called Me 'Disgusting' for Request to Pump Breast Milk," CNN, July 29, 2015, http://www.cnn.com/2015/07/29/politics/trump-breast-pump-statement.

17. Katie Reilly, "Melania Trump: Donald's Words Were 'Unacceptable and Offensive to Me,'" *Fortune*, October 8, 2016, http://fortune.com/2016/10/08/melania-trump-response-donald-trump-leaked-audio.

18. "'I Never Said I'm a Perfect Person,' Trump Says About Lewd Comments," CBS News, October 7, 2016, http://www.cbsnews.com/news/donald-trump-defends-lewd-2005-conversation-about-women-as-locker-room-banter.

19. Callum Borchers, "Melania Trump Defended Her Husband on CNN—But Also Threw Some Shade at Him," *Washington Post*, October 18, 2016, https://www.washingtonpost.com/news/the-fix/wp/2016/10/18/melania-

trump-defended-her-husband-on-cnn-but-also-threw-
some-shade-at-him/?utm_term=.8c462dcba76f.

Chapter 5

1. Philip Rucker, John Wagner, and Greg Miller, "Trump, in
    CIA Visit, Attacks Media for Coverage of His Inaugural
    Crowds." *Washington Post*, January 21, 2017, https://www.
    washingtonpost.com/politics/trump-in-cia-visit-attacks-
    media-for-coverage-of-his-inaugural-crowds/2017/01/21/
    f4574dca-e019-11e6-ad42-f3375f271c9c_story.html?utm_
    term=.a866899ee044.
2. Julie Hirschfeld Davis and Matthew Rosenberg, "With False
    Claims, Trump Attacks Media on Turnout and Intelligence
    Rift," *New York Times,* January 21, 2017, https://www.
    nytimes.com/2017/01/21/us/politics/trump-white-house-
    briefing-inauguration-crowd-size.html.
3. Tom Batchelor, "Donald Trump Responds to Women's
    Marches by Claiming Protestors Didn't Vote," *Independent*,
    January 22, 2017, http://www.independent.co.uk/news/
    world/americas/donald-trump-us-president-women-
    marches-inauguration-protesters-didnt-vote-tweet-
    twitter-a7540141.html.
4. "Melania Trump's White House Snub: Appalling or Good
    Parenting?" BBC, November 21, 2016, http://www.bbc.com/
    news/world-us-canada-38048733.
5. Lauren A. Wright, "Melania Trump Refuses to Act Like a
    First Lady. Good for Her," *Denver Post*, January 19, 2017,
    http://www.denverpost.com/2017/01/19/melania-trump-
    refuses-to-act-like-a-first-lady-good-for-her.
6. Tom Hamburger, "Melania Trump Missed Out on 'Once-
    in-a-Lifetime Opportunity' to Make Millions, Lawsuit
    Says," *Washington Post*, February 7, 2017, https://www.
    washingtonpost.com/politics/melania-trump-missed-out-
    on-once-in-a-lifetime-opportunity-to-make-millions-
    lawsuit-says/2017/02/06/3654f070-ecd0-11e6-9973-
    c5efb7ccfb0d_story.html?utm_term=.98b80fc67638.

7. Kate Bennett, "What's at Stake in Melania Trump Lawsuit: The First Lady's Reputation, Earning Potential," CNN, February 8, 2017, http://www.cnn.com/2017/02/07/politics/melania-trump-lawsuit-earning-potential.

8. Aaron Blake, "What Is an Executive Order? And How Do President Trump's Stack Up?" *Washington Post*, January 27, 2017, https://www.washingtonpost.com/news/the-fix/wp/2017/01/27/what-is-an-executive-order-and-how-do-president-trumps-stack-up/?utm_term=.bb46e1e7484f.

Chapter 6

1. Andrea Gonzalez-Ramirez, "Everything You Ever Wanted to Know About the Role of the First Lady," *Refinery29*, January 18, 2017, http://www.refinery29.com/2017/01/135816/first-lady-role-melania-trump-michelle-obama.

2. Stephanie Mencimer, "Whatever Happened to Melania Trump's Anti-Cyberbullying Campaign?" *Mother Jones*, February 7, 2017, http://www.motherjones.com/politics/2017/02/whatever-happened-melania-trumps-anti-cyberbullying-campaign.

3. Deena Zaru, "The Donald Trump-Rosie O'Donnell Feud: A Timeline," CNN, September 27, 2016, http://www.cnn.com/2015/08/07/politics/donald-trump-rosie-odonnell-feud.

4. Claire Landsbaum, "Donald Trump's Harassment of a Teenage Girl on Twitter Led to Death and Rape Threats," *Cut*, December 9, 2016, http://nymag.com/thecut/2016/12/trumps-harassment-of-an-18-year-old-girl-on-twitter-led-to-death-threats.html.

5. Eli Watkins, "Lady Gaga: Melania Trump Campaigning for Anti-Bullying Is 'Hypocrisy,'" CNN, November 8, 2016, http://www.cnn.com/2016/11/06/politics/lady-gaga-melania-trump-bullying-election-2016.

6. Philip Bump, "Donald Trump Took 5 Different Positions on Abortion in 3 Days," *Washington Post*, April 3, 2016, https://www.washingtonpost.com/news/the-fix/wp/2016/04/03/donald-trumps-ever-shifting-positions-on-abortion/?utm_term=.b8cd9382e043.

GLOSSARY

American Civil Liberties Union (ACLU) A national organization that works to protect individual rights and liberties guaranteed by the Constitution and laws of the United States.

battleground state During a US election, a state that could go in favor of either the Democratic or Republican Party, ultimately determining the outcome of the election.

blind trust A financial arrangement in which an elected official places all business interests in the hands of a third party, thereby eliminating conflicts of interest.

communist Describing a political theory in which everything is owned and operated by the state, theoretically putting all citizens on equal footing within the government and ridding society of social classes.

consensual Relating to the understanding that all parties are in agreement to proceed.

dialect A variation within a language because of region, distance, and evolution of the language over time.

entrepreneur A businessperson who starts and manages a new business.

guerrilla warfare A type of nontraditional warfare that involves sabotage, taking advantage of the environment, and working in secret in a perhaps dishonorable but effective way.

indoctrination The process of instructing a person or group to accept certain beliefs uncritically.

legacy A famous figure's historical significance.

libel A type of defamation expressed through the written word.

misogynistic Clearly expressing an extreme dislike of women or feminine things.

Nova Scotia One of Canada's three Maritime provinces.

plagiarize To borrow, either deliberately or accidentally, someone else's words or ideas without giving proper credit to the original writer.

Republican National Convention (RNC) A series of conventions to nominate presidential candidates of the United States Republican Party.

slander A type of defamation spoken aloud.

subsidy A sum of money given by the government or another entity to assist a business.

supermodel A model whose reach extends beyond the profession of modeling, heightening his or her career to fame and stardom.

Twitter An online social networking service that allows users to post and respond to messages called "tweets" that are restricted to 140 characters.

work visa A written legal document that allows an individual the ability to legally look for and perform work within a specific country different from that individual's country of origin.

FURTHER INFORMATION

Books

Bain, Carolyn, and Steve Fallon. *Lonely Planet Slovenia.* Melbourne, Australia: Lonely Planet, 2016.

Brower, Kate Anderson. *First Women: The Grace and Power of America's Modern First Ladies.* New York: Harper Paperbacks, 2017.

Johnston, David Cay. *The Making of Donald Trump.* Brooklyn, NY: Melville House, 2016.

Websites

Donald Trump's Website
https://www.donaldjtrump.com

The official website of the Trump/Pence presidential campaign and presidency provides some of the latest news, surveys, and issues from the Trump presidency.

Fodor's Slovenia Travel Guide
http://www.fodors.com/world/europe/slovenia

This guide to travel in the European nation of Slovenia can help travelers plan a trip or just read more about the country.

Melania Trump Twitter Feed
https://twitter.com/melaniatrump

Melania Trump's Twitter account provides first-person accounts of the day-to-day happenings of the First Lady.

National First Ladies' Library
http://www.firstladies.org/biographies

The National First Ladies' Library is the official record of past and future United States First Ladies.

The White House
https://www.whitehouse.gov

The official White House website offers biographies of the top people working in the White House and outlines some of the bills and decisions that are on the president's radar.

Video

Melania Trump on Her Life, Marriage, and 2016
https://www.youtube.com/watch?v=XbvGxDmD3dY

In this 2016 interview with MSNBC, Melania Trump talks about her childhood in Slovenia, experiences during the Trump presidential campaign, and life as a mother.

BIBLIOGRAPHY

Alperstein, Robin. "Executive Orders: All Part of the Trump Propaganda/Brand-Building Machine." *Voluble*, January 26, 2017. https://medium.com/voluble/executive-orders-all-part-of-the-trump-propaganda-brand-building-machine-9b4f0c38626a#.fmsap4zgk.

Bates, Daniel, and Clemence Michallon. "Melania Trump Poses Naked for Max Magazine." *Daily Mail*, July 31, 2016. http://www.dailymail.co.uk/news/article-3717333/Melania-Trump-poses-naked-Max-magazine.html.

Brown, Elisha. "How a Freelance Journalist Broke the Melania Trump Plagiarism Story in 3 Tweets." *Vox*, July 21, 2016. http://www.vox.com/2016/7/21/12247504/jarrett-hill-melania-trump-plagiarism.

Caldwell, Alicia A., Chad Day, and Jake Pearson. "Melania Trump Modeled in US Prior to Getting Work Visa." Associated Press, November 5, 2016. https://apnews.com/37dc7aef0ce44077930b7436be7bfd0d.

Collins, Lauren. "The Model American." *New Yorker*, May 9, 2016. http://www.newyorker.com/magazine/2016/05/09/who-is-melania-trump.

Craig, Daniel. "Reactions to Donald Trump's Presidential Announcement Speech." *Philly Voice*, June 16, 2015. http://www.phillyvoice.com/fact-checking-trumps-presidential-speech.

D'Antonio, Michael. "Who Is Donald Trump?" CNN.com, July 10, 2016. http://www.cnn.com/2016/07/10/opinions/donald-trump-biography-michael-dantonio.

Ellison, Sarah. "Inside Ivanka and Tiffany Trump's Complicated Sister Act." *Vanity Fair*, December 22, 2016. http://www. vanityfair.com/news/2016/12/inside-ivanka-trump-and-tiffany-trump-complicated-sister-act.

Fisher, Marc, and Michael Kranish. "The Inside Story of How 'The Apprentice' Rescued Donald Trump." *Fortune*, September 8, 2016. http://fortune.com/2016/09/08/donald-trump-the-apprentice-burnett.

Friedersdorf, Conor. "When Donald Trump Became a Celebrity." *Atlantic*, January 6, 2016. https://www.theatlantic.com/politics/archive/2016/01/the-decade-when-donald-trump-became-a-celebrity/422838.

Geewax, Marilyn. "Trump's Financial Moves in The '90s: 'Genius' Or 'Colossal Failure'?" National Public Radio, October 3, 2016. http://www.npr.org/2016/10/03/496314538/trumps-financial-moves-in-the-90s-genius-or-colossal-failure.

Gonzalez-Ramirez, Andrea. "Everything You Ever Wanted to Know About the Role of the First Lady." *Refinery29*, January 18, 2017. http://www.refinery29.com/2017/01/135816/first-lady-role-melania-trump-michelle-obama.

Horowitz, Jason. "For Donald Trump, Lessons from a Brother's Suffering." *New York Times*, January 2, 2016. https://www.nytimes.com/2016/01/03/us/politics/for-donald-trump-lessons-from-a-brothers-suffering.html?_r=0.

———. "Fred Trump Taught His Son the Essentials of Showboating Self-Promotion." *New York Times*, August 12, 2016. https://www.nytimes.com/2016/08/13/us/politics/fred-donald-trump-father.html.

Iocob, Ivona. "Melania Trump's Flops Go Beyond Her Convention Speech." *Forbes*, July 19, 2016. https://www.forbes.com/sites/ivonaiacob/2016/07/19/melania-trump-convention-speech/#4f9a87d44b1f.

Ioffe, Julia. "Melania Trump on Her Rise, Her Family Secrets, and Her True Political Views: "Nobody Will Ever Know." *GQ*, April 27, 2016. http://www.gq.com/story/melania-trump-gq-interview.

"Ivana Trump." *Hello!* Accessed February 20, 2017. http://us.hellomagazine.com/profiles/ivana-trump.

James, Sabrina. "Melania Trump Juggles Motherhood, Marriage, and a Career Just Like Us." *Parenting*, 2011. Accessed March 5, 2017. http://www.parenting.com/blogs/hip-mama/melania-trump-shares-her-1-parenting-tip-and-secrets-lasting-marriage.

Johnston, David Cay. "Meet Freidrich—Pimp, Profiteer and Patriarch of the Trump Line." *Daily Beast*, August 2, 2016. http://www.thedailybeast.com/articles/2016/08/02/meet-freidrich-pimp-profiteer-and-patriarch-of-the-trump-line.html.

McCarthy, Ciara, and Claire Phipps. "Election Results Timeline: How the Night Unfolded." *Guardian*, November 9, 2016. https://www.theguardian.com/us-news/2016/nov/08/presidential-election-updates-trump-clinton-news.

"Melania Trump." Biography.com, January 24, 2017. http://www.biography.com/people/melania-trump-812016.

Moskowitz, Peter. "What Happened to Melania Trump's Caviar Skincare Line?" *Racked*, August 22, 2016. http://www.racked.com/2016/8/22/12556786/melania-trump-caviar-skincare-lawsuit.

O'Harrow, Robert, Jr. "Trump's Bad Bet: How Too Much Debt Drove His Biggest Casino Aground." *Washington Post*, January 18, 2016. https://www.washingtonpost.com/investigations/trumps-bad-bet-how-too-much-debt-drove-his-biggest-casino-aground/2016/01/18/f67cedc2-9ac8-11e5-8917-653b65c809eb_story.html?utm_term=.bf9c495794ef.

Orth, Maureen. "The Heart of the Deal: The Love Story of Marla Maples and Donald Trump." *Vanity Fair*, November 1, 1990. http://www.vanityfair.com/news/1990/11/marla-maples-donald-trump-relationship.

Pilon, Mary. "Donald Trump's Immigrant Mother." *New Yorker*, June 24, 2016. http://www.newyorker.com/news/news-desk/donald-trumps-immigrant-mother.

Pozar, Bojan, and Igor Omerza. *Melania Trump: The Inside Story; The Potential First Lady*. Ljubljana, Slovenia: Zalozba Ombo d.o.o., 2016.

Reed, Sam. "6 Things to Know About Barron Trump, the Youngest of Donald's Heirs." *Hollywood Reporter*, November 22, 2016. http://www.hollywoodreporter.com/news/6-things-know-barron-trump-youngest-donalds-heirs-949947.

Ritman, Alex. "GQ Editor Recalls Donald Trump Wife's Controversial Nude Photo Shoot." *Hollywood Reporter*, March 25, 2016. http://www.hollywoodreporter.com/news/gq-editor-recalls-donald-trump-878336.

Roberts, Hannah. "Is This America's Next First Lady?" *Daily Mail*, October 29, 2015. http://www.dailymail.co.uk/news/article-3279399/Will-Lady-Melania-Trump-s-extraordinary-journey-card-carrying-Communist-s-daughter-teenage-model-White-House-favorite-s-wife-revealed.html.

Sebastian, Michael. "29 Times Donald Trump Has Been Completely Insulting to Women." *Cosmopolitan*, October 21, 2016. http://www.cosmopolitan.com/politics/news/a44629/donald-trump-insults-women.

Stojanovic, Dusan. "Melania Trump's Slovenia Has Become a Tourist Hotspot." Associated Press, August 15, 2016. http://bigstory.ap.org/article/ec973eee0c3e40099665ff21b791539f/melania-trumps-slovenia-has-become-tourist-hotspot.

Stoynoff, Natasha. "Donald Trump Weds Melania Knauss." *People*, January 23, 2005. http://people.com/celebrity/donald-trump-weds-melania-knauss.

Summerfield, Luke. "How to Build a Brand That Attracts Die-Hard Followers." *Entrepreneur*, April 4, 2014. https://www.entrepreneur.com/article/232805.

Trebay, Guy. "Melania Trump, the Silent Partner." *New York Times*, September 30, 2015. https://www.nytimes.com/2015/10/01/fashion/melania-trump-the-silent-partner.html?mtrref=undefined&gwh=E65EA39D0C9E1E978EF9FF8E35D3964C&gwt=pay&assetType=nyt_now.

Twohey, Megan, and Michael Barbaro. "Two Women Say Donald Trump Touched Them Inappropriately." *New York Times*, October 12, 2016. https://www.nytimes.com/2016/10/13/us/politics/donald-trump-women.html?smprod=nytcore-iphone&smid=nytcore-iphone-share&_r=0.

"War for Slovenia 1991." Slovenia 2001. Accessed March 3, 2017. http://www.slovenija2001.gov.si/10years/path/war.

Weill, Kelly. "How to Look Like Trump's Third Wife Using Her Half-Off Skincare Line and Knock-Off Jewelry." *Daily Beast*, October 10, 2015. http://www.thedailybeast.com/articles/2015/10/10/how-to-look-like-trump-s-third-wife-using-her-half-off-skincare-line-and-knock-off-jewelry.html.

Wilkin, Sam. "How Donald Trump Got Rich." *Business Insider*, March 26, 2016. http://www.businessinsider.com/how-donald-trump-got-rich-2016-3.

Zadrozny, Brandy. "Donald Trump Made Out with Marla Maples as She Delivered His Child." *Daily Beast*, September 5, 2016. http://www.thedailybeast.com/articles/2016/09/05/donald-trump-made-out-with-marla-maples-as-she-delivered-his-child.html.

INDEX

ABOUT THE AUTHOR

Bethany Bryan is a professional writer, copy editor, and editor. She enjoys studying and writing about history and visiting presidential museums. She has published books with Scholastic, Adams Media, and Rosen Publishing.